THIS IS *Love*

Becky Combee

Illustrations by Wayne Combee

THIS IS LOVE
   By Becky Combee
Published by Becky Combee Ministries, Inc.
P.O. Box 3283
Lakeland, FL 33802-3283
Beckycombeeministries.com

ISBN-13: 978-0983278313
ISBN-10: 0983278318

All illustrations were drawn by Becky's husband, Wayne Combee. Cover art by Suzanne D. Williams.

Unless otherwise noted, all Scripture references were taken from the *King James Version* of the Bible.

Scripture notations marked AMP were taken from the Amplified® Bible, Copyright © 1954, 1958, 1962, 1964, 1965, 1987 by The Lockman Foundation. Used by permission. <www.lockman.org>.

Scripture notations marked ASV were taken from the *American   Standard   Version*   from <www.biblegateway.com>.

Scripture notations marked BBE were taken from *1965*

Scripture notations marked WEY were taken from the *1912 Weymouth New Testament* from <www.e-sword.net>. Accessed 17 May 2011.

Definitions marked *Strong's* were taken from Strong, James, S.T.D., LL.D., *Strong's Exhaustive Concordance of the Bible*, (Peabody, Mass.: Hendrickson Publishers)

Definitions marked *Thayer's* were taken from *Thayer's Greek Definitions* from <www.e-sword.net>.

Definitions marked *Vine's* were taken from Vine, W.E., M.A., *Vine's Expository Dictionary of New Testament Words,* Unabridged ed. (McLean, Va.: MacDonald Publishing Company)

Definitions marked *Webster's*, 1959, were taken from *Webster's New Collegiate Dictionary*, 2d ed. (Springfield, Mass.: G. & C. Merriam Co., 1959)

Definitions marked *Webster's*, 1828, were taken from Webster, Noah, *An American Dictionary of the English Language*, 1st ed. (San Francisco, Calif.: Foundation For American Christian Education, 2002)

TABLE OF CONTENTS

.

DEDICATION

We dedicate this book to our daughter, Suzanne. Month after month, she patiently worked with our text to perfect the grammar and vocabulary so that it communicates God's message of love. Without her tireless effort, we would still be stuck in the mire of punctuation. We love you lots.

Mom and Dad

INTRODUCTION

When my mother asked me to write the introduction to this book, it was at the end of a long day and I was more than a little burnt out. All I could remember about love was a funny ditty my grandfather used to say:

Love is a funny thing shaped like a lizard.

Goes all around your heart and gobbles at your gizzard.

Now in my family, this poem has always provided a good laugh, especially the time my father chose to quote it to my mother in front of her friends. However, I am aware it has little to do with the message of the book, so I left that day and began meditating on the love of God.

Today, I find myself overwhelmed. How wide, how high, and how deep is the love of God! In our earthly lives, epitaphs and statues are erected to honor love. We dedicate palaces and gardens to our love. We spend thousands of dollars and expend hours of labor to express love. Yet in comparison to what God did, these all seem to pale.

Because He loved us SO MUCH, God gave us His HIGHEST and BEST gift.

LOVE IS FUNNY

Jesus came as the ultimate sacrifice of love. His death and resurrection are the fullest expression of God's desire. Jesus laid down his life for even the worst person in the annals of history. That is IMMENSE love! And He came to restore the closeness, fellowship, and intimacy, man had with God in the garden. He came so that we could call, and God would answer.

> God's GREAT love crosses all barriers of time, race, religion, or denomination to offer eternal life, abundance, and joy to any who will believe.

It touches us no matter who we are, how smart we've become, or how much we have failed. God's love in us is SO FULL that it cannot but overflow from our lives into the lives of those around us. We now love because He loved first.

I pray in reading this book that you will realize the true grandeur of God's amazing love. For the principles of the Word placed here have the capacity to change your life forever, if you will let them, if you will practice them. God's love in your life will revolutionize the way you think and alter the way you act. You will truly never be the same.

Suzanne D. Williams

1

GOD'S LOVE IS SO BIG!

---

*For God **so loved** the world, that He gave His only begotten Son, that whosoever believeth in Him should not perish, but have everlasting life (John 3:16).*

"God so loved the world!" [1] What a powerful declaration by our Lord Jesus Christ! What glorious words of comfort! God loved us! We were His enemies, ungodly and weak, yet He loved us. He loved us even when we were sinners, and through His great love, we have been rescued from sin. This dramatic rescue is for every man, every woman, and every child. **Jesus' sacrifice has opened the door of salvation to all the world.** Today, no man or spirit being can shut that door. It is guarded by our resurrected and ascended Lord. It is the door of eternal life.

The magnitude of God's love for every man is voiced by one word from John 3:16 – "God SO loved the world." With the small word "SO" we see the expanse of God's love, its "breadth, and length, and depth, and height." [2]

---

[1] Jn 3:16
[2] Eph 3:18

Isn't that amazing? The extent of God's love declared in one word! Yet no other word can more adequately express the dimensions of His love.

The love of God for man is simply **SO** *big!*

The limitless magnitude of God's love reminds me of the many times my husband, Wayne, and I traveled across the Atlantic Ocean. Without a doubt, it is SO big. On one trip from Russia, through Scotland, and home to the United States, I became acutely aware of the size of this *great* ocean. Three hours from the border of the United States, I was ready to get out of the plane.

I teased our son, who was with us, saying, "I'm tired. I have to get out now." The ocean went on and on and on and on. It seemed to grow bigger and bigger. It was SO big. Yet **its grand size cannot be compared to the endless horizons of God's love.**

This SO love of God is also reminiscent of the great animals of God's creation. On a visit to the zoo, we watched an elephant giving rides. It didn't matter if the rider was a child or an adult. Compared to the elephant they were SO small, and he was SO big.

That same day, the elephant used a water hose to take a drink. I am still amazed because he drank continually for a very long time. This giant of God's creation had enormous capacity. However, his vast thirst does not challenge the bounty of God's love.

ETERNAL LIFE

God's immeasurable love came to earth through Jesus Christ. We recognize this love because Jesus, His only Son "laid down His life for us." [3]

Jesus' loving sacrifice unveiled the Father's love, love SO grand that Jesus came down from heaven to hang on an "old rugged cross." [4] He left heaven's glory to walk earth's dusty roads and die on Golgotha's hill. In death, He bore our sin, defeated our enemy, Satan, and secured our freedom. Through Him we have eternal life.

God's promise of everlasting, or eternal, life through Jesus' death is often voiced in the Scripture. In a conversation with Nicodemus, a ruler of the Jews, Jesus said:

Whosoever believeth in Him should not perish, but have eternal life. [5]

He repeated this to the Jews who plotted His death. We read His words in John 5:24.

---

[3] 1Jn 3:16
[4] "The Old Rugged Cross," Words and Music: George Bennard, 1913, <www.cyberhymnal.org/htm/o/r/oruggedc.htm>, Accessed 17 May 2011.
[5] Jn 3:15

He that heareth my word, and believeth on him that sent me, hath everlasting life. [6]

Jesus also spoke of it to the woman at the well in Samaria, inviting her to drink from a well of water "springing up into everlasting life." [7]
Over and over again, our Lord Jesus Christ heralds God's eternal provision. The inspired writers of the gospels also testified of eternal life after Jesus' death and Resurrection.
In 1 John 5:11, the apostle John declares:

God hath given to us eternal life, and this life is in his Son.

He states it again in a following passage. "He that believeth on the Son hath everlasting life." [8]
The apostle Paul adds his witness, saying:

The gift of God is eternal life through Jesus Christ our Lord. [9]

---

[6] Jn 5:24
[7] Jn 4:14
[8] Jn 3:36
[9] Ro 6:23

What glorious proclamations of truth!

What is "eternal life?" When teaching Bible classes, I often ask this question and the usual answer is, "to live forever." But, as I tell the students, a sinner lives forever, yet he does not have eternal life. Surely, eternal life is more than length of life! Our relationship with God must be bigger than an endless expanse of time.

The apostle John gives light on eternal life, saying:

For the life was manifested, and we have seen it. [10]

I love the word "manifested." It reminds me of the tantalizing smell of food Mother would cook, particularly on Sunday. When you opened the front door of our house after church, the aroma of food simmering on the stove sent good news to your senses. Lunch was going to be delicious! Yet only after you dashed to the stove and lifted the lid on the saucepan did you see what awaited you.

This is the testimony of the apostle John. "Lifting the lid" on eternal life, he declares, "He who gives life was shown to us." [11] Certainly, he was introducing us to Jesus, "the way, the truth, and the life."[12]

When we acknowledge the Resurrection of Jesus and confess Him as Lord, we receive His life. The apostle Peter explains further that at that moment we share the divine nature.

---

[10] 1 Jn 1:2
[11] 1Jn 1:2, NCV
[12] Jn 14:6

GOOD NEWS
IS MANIFESTED

The *Contemporary English Version* translates Peter's words:

God made great and marvelous promises, so that his nature would become part of us. [13]

This is magnificent news! God's nature, the life of God, now dwells in us. Or we can say it this way: *The SO love of*

---

[13] 2Pe 1:4

God has given us the life of the Eternal One.

ABUNDANT LIFE

Eternal life is ABUNDANT life! Jesus shared this truth when He said:

I am come that they might have life, and that they might have it more abundantly. [14]

Strong's Exhaustive Concordance of the Bible describes abundant life as "beyond measure, exceeding abundantly above, superfluous or excessive." [15] **It is life superior in quantity and quality.**

At a child's birthday party, we must often decide between quantity and quality. When choosing $20.00 of party favors, we can purchase 20 items at $1.00 each or 10 items at $2.00 each. The one-dollar gift is cheaper, and we will have plenty. The two-dollar favor is better quality, but we can purchase only ten.

Do we need quantity or quality? We must decide. **I am so glad eternal life is measured by God's SO love in both quantity AND quality. We don't have to choose!**

The word "abundance" reminds me of eating Thanksgiving dinner with the Combee family. On this special occasion, our large family gathered to eat and thank the Lord for His blessings. My husband's parents, now

---

[14] Jn 10:10
[15] G4053 *Strong's*

gloriously in heaven, were farmers, so each meal included bountiful "fruit" from the garden. I certainly can't name every dish, but you can be sure there was more than enough. From chicken and dumplings, chicken and dressing, baked ham, green beans, steamed okra, creamed corn, sliced tomatoes, collard greens, and black-eyed peas to coconut cake, pound cake with strawberries, fruitcake, and chocolate pie, the meal was "exceeding abundantly above all that [you] ask or think." [16] It was beyond measure. It was wonderful.

God's unlimited, eternal life is wonderful, surpassing our greatest expectations. Its overwhelming magnitude prompts us to ask why. Why did God offer this abundant, eternal life to man? In Ephesians 2:4-5, the apostle Paul gives the answer:

[God's] great love ... hath quickened us together with Christ.

The word "quickened" means "to make one alive together." [17] We are quickened, or made alive, because of God's great love.

Abundant, eternal life springs from God's SO love.

[16] Eph 3:20
[17] G4806 *Thayers'*

YOU MUST BE BORN AGAIN

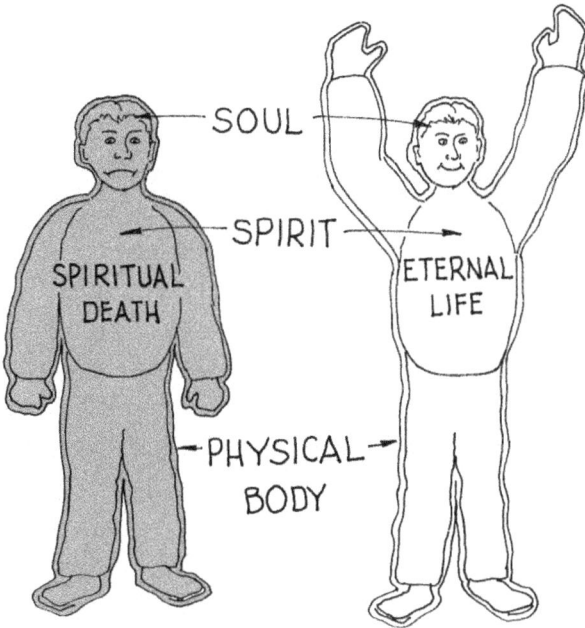

SOUL

SPIRIT

SPIRITUAL
DEATH

ETERNAL
LIFE

PHYSICAL
BODY

SPIRIT, SOUL, AND BODY

Eternal life changes man. According to 1 Thessalonians 5:23, man is a unity of three parts: spirit, soul, and body. He is a spirit being who possesses a soul and lives in a physical body.

When we confess Jesus as Savior and Lord, our spirit is recreated, or born again.

Jesus taught this truth in John 3:6-7 when he contrasted the physical birth of man with his spiritual birth.

He stated:

> *That which is born of the flesh is flesh; and that which is born of the Spirit is spirit. Marvel not that I said unto thee, ye must be born again.*

These words describe the recreation of man's spirit by the power of the Holy Spirit.

I have seen Jesus' words, "that which is born of the flesh is flesh," visually portrayed in my own life. Anyone who knew my mother instantly recognizes me because I look so much like her. Frequently I hear someone say, "You must be Juanita's daughter." My fleshly resemblance to her is obvious. My resemblance to God should be as apparent.

> *Through Jesus Christ, I have God's nature. I am a spirit being, born again, changed and new. My life now reflects His life.*

The apostle Paul acknowledges this in 2 Corinthians 5:17. He says:

> *Therefore if any man be in Christ, he is a new creature.*

Although we would not use the word "creature" in reference to people, we understand that he means we are new in spirit. *The Message* translation of this verse states it this way:

Now we look inside, and what we see is that anyone united with the Messiah gets a fresh start, is created new. The old life is gone; a new life burgeons!

What a glorious declaration from the Word of God!

This truth from God's Word became real to me when I was nine years old. We had a guest speaker on Sunday, a friend of my parents. As he taught God's Word, I became more and more aware that I was a sinner, that I did not have God's life. That day, fearfully, I walked to the front of our church and declared Jesus my Lord and Savior. At that moment, I was born again. I was changed!

Every man accepts God's offer of salvation for himself. With the words of his mouth, he recognizes Jesus as the resurrected Savior and proclaims Him as his Lord. This heart-felt commitment establishes him as a new creation with eternal life.

The Holy Spirit speaks this truth in Romans 10:9.

If you confess with your mouth the Lord Jesus and believe in your heart that God has raised Him from the dead, you will be saved. [18]

This declaration of salvation is absolute. You WILL be saved!

[18] NKJV

It is not a half-hearted, maybe so, hope-so, or could-be offer.

Jesus is the Lamb of God crucified for sinners. When He arose from death, sin was conquered, and Satan was defeated. This victory over death is for everyone who will confess Jesus as Lord.

Every man can have eternal life TODAY. TODAY is the day of salvation! TODAY, we confess Jesus as Lord and we are born again.

The proclamation of 2 Corinthians 6:2 gloriously declares:

Behold, now is the accepted time; behold, now is the day of salvation.

Oh, how amazing it is to be saved NOW! How wonderful it is to have eternal life NOW! What a lavish provision! [19] TODAY, through God's wondrous love, we are born again!

---

[19] 1Jn 3:1 NIV

Scriptures for Meditation:

(John 5:24) Verily, verily, I say unto you, He that heareth my word, and believeth on him that sent me, hath everlasting life, and shall not come into condemnation; but is passed from death unto life.

(John 10:10) The thief cometh not, but for to steal, and to kill, and to destroy: I am come that they might have life, and that they might have it more abundantly.

(2 Corinthians 5:17) Therefore if any man be in Christ, he is a new creature: old things are passed away; behold, all things are become new.

2

LOVE ONE ANOTHER

---

*A new commandment I give to you, that you love one another; as I have loved you, that you also **love one another** (John 13:34).*

God's infinite love came to us through the Lord Jesus Christ, and it is displayed in our lives as we "love one another." Jesus explained this when He said:

By this shall all men know that ye are my disciples, if ye have love one to another. [1]

His command to love each other is the ruling principle of our walk with God. As we heed His words, our lives influence others.

In his first epistle, the apostle John spoke often of God's love. One of my favorite verses is 1 John 4:11:

---

[1] Jn 13:35

Beloved, if God so loved us, we ought also to love one another.

I love the word "ought." In *Webster's New Collegiate Dictionary,* the word "ought" means:

"to be bound, as by practical duty, by moral laws, or by conscience."

It is further defined, "to be necessary, becoming, or expedient." According to these definitions, it is necessary and expedient that we love one another. Our conscience commands it as a duty. Because God loved us, we ought to love one another.

JESUS

Jesus is our example of God's great love. He humbled Himself to fulfill the Father's will, [2] giving His life as "a ransom for many."[3] His sacrificial death and compassionate life reveal God's commitment to man and demonstrate our responsibility to love one another.

The Old Covenant unveils the birth, death, and resurrection of Jesus, God's greatest gift of love. Many centuries before Jesus' birth in Bethlehem, the prophet Isaiah announced:

---

[2] Php 2:7 NLT
[3] Mt 20:28

16

For unto us a child is born, unto us a son is given. [4]

He described Jesus as:

Wonderful, Counsellor, The mighty God, The everlasting Father, The Prince of Peace. [5]

He brought our attention to Jesus' death and proclaimed Him "a man of sorrows." [6] He noted that Jesus was:

wounded for our transgressions

The psalmist furthers our vision of Jesus' death. His prophetic words state:

They pierced my hands and my feet. [7]

---

[4] Isa 9:6
[5] Isa 9:6
[6] Isa 53:3
[7] Ps 22:16

Job foresaw Jesus' Resurrection with the proclamation:

I know that my redeemer liveth. [8]

Each of these servants held in their heart a measure of God's plan to unveil His Son to the world. They could not access the fullness of God's grace but proclaimed God's glorious plan of redemption one piece at a time.

The true magnitude of God's sacrifice was not fully revealed until Jesus' blood sealed the New Covenant.

At that time, the mystery of the Old Covenant, with its vast body of laws and commandments, was unraveled, and the portrait, drawn by these prophets, priests, and kings, emerged. The picture of salvation, growing through the ages of time, was complete.

THE OLD AND NEW COVENANTS

The Old Covenant with its animal sacrifices was God's pattern for a new and better covenant. The Day of Atonement, which Israel celebrated every year, graphically portrayed Jesus' death to establish this New Covenant.

On the Day of Atonement, the priest entered into the Most Holy Place offering the blood of animals for his sins

---

[8] Job 19:25

and the sins of the people. This sacrifice depicted the blood of Jesus shed for the redemption of man.

> *The blood of Jesus is the guarantee, the foundation, of God's New Covenant plan to "put away," or "blot out," [9] sin.*

The Greek word translated "blot" means, "to smear, obliterate and wipe away." [10] With His sacrifice, Jesus "put away" sin. He victoriously declared:

Their sins and iniquities will I remember no more.
[11]

The animal sacrifices of the Old Covenant did not have the power to "blot out" sin. They simply covered sin as a glove covers a man's hand.

This is substantiated by the writer of Hebrews:

For it is not possible that the blood of bulls and of goats should take away sins. [12]

---

[9] Ac 3:19
[10] G1813, *Strong's*
[11] Heb 10:17
[12] Heb 10:4

The only blood that can blot out sin is Jesus' blood.

Together, the Old and New Testaments communicate the fullness of God's great plan of salvation. While the Old Covenant pointed to Jesus who would die for man's sin, the New Covenant follows our Lord to the cross to put away sin by the sacrifice of himself."[13]

The Old provided the continual sacrifice of animals to

---

[13] Heb 9:26

"cover" man's sin, [14] but the New unveils the sacrifice of Jesus to remove sin. [15]

Because of Jesus, the glories of the Old Covenant, with its pictures of death and resurrection, yielded to a more glorious New Covenant. [16]

Every command of the Old Covenant achieved its purpose through Jesus' life. Jesus explained this to His disciples in the Sermon on the Mount. He said:

Think not that I am come to destroy the law, or the prophets: I am not come to destroy, but to fulfil. [17]

By His death and Resurrection, He completed the Old Covenant, sealed its record, and opened the door to the New. The writer of Hebrews verifies this truth:

In that He saith, a new covenant, He hath made the first old. Now that which decayeth and waxeth old is ready to vanish away. [18]

---

[14] Lev 4:31,35;5:18;6:7, H3722, "atonement," *Strong's*
[15] Ac 3:19
[16] 2Co 3:7-11
[17] Mt 5:17
[18] Heb 8:13

Truly, the Old Covenant has surrendered to God's magnificent New Covenant.

GOD'S LAW OF LOVE

After the birth of the New Covenant, the Old Covenant, with its many laws and sacrifices, ceased to govern the children of God. This transition from the Old Covenant laws of Moses to God's New Testament principle is frequently misunderstood, but God's Old Covenant laws have submitted to a new law, the law of love. Jesus proclaimed:

A new commandment I give unto you, That ye love one another; as I have loved you, that ye also love one another. [19]

In his letter to the church at Rome, the apostle Paul compares this new law of love to the Ten Commandments. He explains that the law of love summarizes these Old Covenant commandments. [20] This truth is revealed to the churches in Galatia as well. The apostle Paul writes:

For all the law is fulfilled in one word, even in this; Thou shalt love thy neighbor as thyself. [21]

---

[19] Jn 13:34
[20] Ro 13:9 ASV
[21] Gal 5:14

22

If we obey this principle of love, we fulfill the Old Testament commandments.

Every Christian can faithfully follow God's command of love because God has placed His loving nature in our heart.

In Romans 5:5, the apostle Paul testifies:

The love of God is shed abroad in our hearts by the Holy Ghost.

The phrase "shed abroad" is defined in the original Greek language as "to pour forth, to gush out, to run greedily out". [22] As we yield to God's love, it pours from our hearts into the lives of others. It "gushes out" of our spirit like water from a bubbling spring.

This outpouring of love reminds me of the big land rush often seen in western movies. At the sound of a gun, people desiring land run hastily to claim ownership. Similarly, God's love rushes from His children to demonstrate His goodness. It runs beyond selfishness and plants the flag of service to others. It rushes past hatred and overcomes strife with the strength of God's peace. God's love incapacitates jealousy, overthrows irritation, and dissolves unkindness.

When God's love floods our lives, we are victorious.

---

[22] G1632, *Strong's*

The love of God must continually operate in our lives. It is never optional or expendable, nor does it ebb-and-flow like the vast waves of the ocean. It always dominates us. **Because we are His ambassadors, we constantly love others as He loved us.**

THE LOVE OF GOD POURS OUT

As we demonstrate His love:

_____

All men know that we are His disciples. [23]

_____

This is the command of the Scripture, and it is our desire. With our heart we declare, "Beloved, let us love one another!" [24]

Scriptures for Meditation:

(John 13:34-35) A new commandment I give unto you, That ye love one another; as I have loved you, that ye also love one another. By this shall all men know that ye are my disciples, if ye have love one to another.

(Romans 5:5) And hope maketh not ashamed; because the love of God is shed abroad in our hearts by the Holy Ghost which is given unto us.

(Romans 13:8-10) Owe no man any thing, but to love one another: for he that loveth another hath fulfilled the law.

_____

[23] Jn 13:35, author's paraphrase
[24] 1Jn 4:7

3

FLESH LIKES!

For the flesh lusteth against the Spirit, and the Spirit against the flesh: and these are contrary the one to the other: so that ye cannot do the things that ye would (Galatians 5:17).

The day we were born again, God's loving nature was poured into our re-created spirit. This love constrains us and compels us to imitate Him. It urges us to "walk in love."[1]

I love the word "walk" because walking is ordinary. Everyone can walk and should walk unless there has been a disabling accident or disease. The Word of God does not ask us to "crawl," or "leap," or "run" because it would not reflect the ability of each Christian. We are simply asked to "walk." But here is a word of caution, our flesh will not "walk in love." It will promote itself and override love's principles.

The decisions of our flesh are prompted by natural, human love. This love depends on our physical senses and

---

[1] Eph 5:2

a mind void of God's thoughts. We say, "I don't feel like it," "I don't want to," and "I'll do as I please." God's love moves far beyond these selfish emotions. Our human impulses vacillate from moment to moment and day to day because they lean on the instability of the flesh.

The love of God, resident in our spirit, is steadfast and unmovable. It is poured into our lives by our God, who cannot change.

Strong's Exhaustive Concordance of the Bible says God's love embraces:

"judgment and the deliberate assent of the will as a matter of principle, duty, and propriety." [2]

This means, **God's love does not depend on our feelings but on our choice.** We disregard fleshly commands, and honor God's command to "love one another."

When we do, His love floods our lives like a river after spring rains.

LOVE IN ACTION

The apostle Paul emphasizes the importance of God's love and the ineffectiveness of our fleshly response in 1 Corinthians 13.

---

[2] G5368, *Strong's*

In verse one of the *New King James Version*, He declares:

Though I speak with the tongues of men and of angels, but have not love, I have become sounding brass, or a clanging cymbal.

Isn't it interesting to note that we might speak eloquently in heavenly and earthly languages, and yet not be heard or understood? Our words, destitute of love, are as inaudible as if we had spoken in the presence of trumpeting brass instruments and clanging cymbals. The gentle song of love, flowing across our heart, silences all the noise.

The Scriptures, through the apostle Paul, speaking to Ephesus, identifies what fleshly actions will override God's love.

We read:

Let all bitterness, and wrath, and anger, and clamour, and evil speaking, be put away from you, with all malice. [3]

These volatile feelings magnify the flesh and, ultimately, hinder the ability of God's love.

---

[3] Eph 4:31

INAUDIBLE WORDS

In a similar voice, the apostle Paul declares to the Colossians:

Put off all these; anger, wrath, malice, blasphemy, filthy communication out of your mouth. [4]

---

[4] Col 3:8

We upend the majesty of God's love by speaking words of the flesh.

Words of pride and selfishness are damaging, yet their power pales in the face of God's love. **God's love magnifies Him, whereas the flesh always speaks with self-interest** and in supposed perfection.

It says, "I am NEVER," or "I can ALWAYS."

The love of God, on the other hand, directs man's attention to the sacrifice of our Lord and Savior and His love for all men. It always glorifies our magnificent Father.

In verse two of this marvelous chapter in 1 Corinthians, we have another important revelation about God's love.

It states:

And though I have the gift of prophecy, and understand all mysteries and all knowledge, and though I have all faith, so that I could remove mountains, but have not love, I am nothing. [5]

Can you imagine manifesting the gift of prophecy, possessing remarkable insight, and having great faith yet being insignificant? We might envy a person who understands every mystery. We would treasure the companionship of someone with phenomenal knowledge

---

[5] NKJV

and perfect faith.

But the final words of this verse strike our spirit:

If I do not have love, then I am nothing. [6]

What does this mean?

The answer is revealed in 1 Corinthians 13:13. Here the Holy Spirit speaks.

And now abide faith, hope, love, these three; but the greatest of these is love. [7]

These great forces of faith, hope, and love fill our heart with joy. How marvelous is man's faith in God and His Word! Hope is equally important, for it provides the confident expectation that propels faith forward. Yet notice, faith and hope are not the greatest works of God.

The greatest attribute of God and His greatest gift to man is love. Love forms the foundation of faith and hope.

The flesh operates outside of God's love. It boasts of knowledge it has gained and applauds its own

---

[6] NCV
[7] NKJV

achievements. It brags about words of prophecy its spoken. But Jesus said:

The flesh profits me nothing. [8]

The spirit of man filled with God's love is the principle of man's success. We are "nothing," ineffective and helpless in God's kingdom if the flesh controls our lives. First Corinthians 13:3 declares:

And though I bestow all my goods to feed the poor, and though I give my body to be burned, but have not love, it profits me nothing. [9]

Here, we see a man of great generosity. His financial sacrifice is unprecedented in measure because he has given his substance and his life for others. How sad it is, then, that the magnitude of his gesture is unprofitable!

As Christians, we can give away every possession. We can open our hands until every need is met and all of our goods are gone. Yet **without the love of God enveloping our actions, our gifts have no merit.**

The flesh cries, "Look at me. See what I have done." It flaunts its wealth and the amount it has given. In contrast, the heart of love weeps when every resource is exhausted.

---

[8] Jn 6:63 NKJV
[9] NKJV

It works in humility and obedience before our great God. The motivation of our every word and deed should be love.

THE FLESH

The love of God must dominate our spirit man, flow from our lips in kind words, and manifest itself in our behavior. **We cannot allow our flesh to take us away from God's wonderful plan for us.** Instead, we follow God's instructions to crucify, or sacrifice, our flesh. When we crucify our flesh, we simply refuse the voice of its demands.

The apostle Paul spoke of his own flesh, saying:

But I keep under my body, and bring it into subjection. [10]

It seems unrealistic that this great man of the gospel would find it necessary to bring his body into subjection, but his words confirm his sacrifice.

This sacrifice is God's requirement for every Christian. The Word of God declares:

For I know that in me (that is, in my flesh,) dwelleth no good thing. [11]

---

[10] 1 Co 9:27
[11] Ro 7:18

What a powerful revelation! Our flesh must be crucified because it cannot accomplish "good things."

The apostle Paul's testimony to the churches in Galatia further enhances our understanding. In chapter five of this letter, he contrasts the cravings of our flesh and the desires of our spirit. He says:

For the flesh lusteth against the Spirit, and the Spirit against the flesh: and these are contrary the one to the other. [12]

The word "lust" in the Greek language means "a longing, especially for what is forbidden." [13] This sounds an instant alarm. We cannot, we must not, be driven by the urges of our flesh.

The path of victory is to "walk in the Spirit," [14] and "be led of the Spirit." [15] This means our human spirit follows the Holy Spirit as He directs our hearts in submission to God and His Word.

This conflict between the flesh and the spirit reminds me of a battle we had, years ago, between our phone and our computer. Every time we answered the phone, the computer quit working. The phone would ring, and we would answer. Then suddenly, the phone would go dead, and the computer would shut down.

---

[12] Gal 5:17
[13] G1939, *Strong's*
[14] Gal 5:16,25
[15] Gal 5:18

I don't have to tell you that the phone should not control the computer.

This is also true of our flesh. It has no authority over our spirit.

One of our friends will tease, "Flesh likes. Flesh likes." I love that example of this struggle between flesh and spirit because I understand the insistence of fleshly desires. The flesh is impatient, selfish, and envious of others. It enjoys anger and rejoices in pride. These actions do not please God, our Father.

But we have good news! **The power of God's great love restrains these fleshly behaviors.**

In 2 Corinthians 5:14, we read:

For the love of Christ constraineth us.

When something is constrained, it is "confined or held back." [16] I remember an argument I almost caused one day. I was particularly tired and started to express my opinion on a matter, unkindly, when God's love constrained me. Oh, thank God for His supernatural love. My spirit rose up and choked my inappropriate words.

God's love is like a seed. As we nurture the seed of God's love, it arrests those feelings that cause us to REACT.

---

[16] *Webster's*, 1959

We are to ACT like God, not REACT in the flesh.

However, we cannot restrain our words and behavior through personal willpower. We may think to ourselves, "I will be kind. I will be kind. I will be kind." But no matter how determined we are, we will soon say, "I'll tell you one thing, you better not do that again!" **Sadly, persistence and self-effort will always fail.**

PLANTING
LOVE

We exclaim with the apostle Paul:

O wretched man that I am! who shall deliver me from the body of this death? [17]

Flooded with grief and despair, we cry out to God, "Is there any help for us?"
With gratitude, we hear Paul's triumphant answer.

Thank God! The answer is in Jesus Christ our Lord. [18]

What big, big news! **Through the death and Resurrection of Jesus Christ, we are victorious.**
Our victory began the day we confessed Jesus as our Lord. We accepted His death for our sin and became children of God. We became "new creatures" [19] with His life and nature. The Spirit of God now dwells in each of us, and He is working mightily to help us.
As He assists us, the demands of the flesh for ascendancy and control are unsuccessful.
The Word of God announces this comforting news.

---

[17] Ro 7:24
[18] Ro 7:25 NLT
[19] 2 Co 5:17

If by the Spirit you put to death the deeds of the body, you will live. [20]

This means the rebellious ways of our flesh CAN be conquered and overthrown. This is wonderful! **God has come to us by His Holy Spirit, who enables us to subdue our flesh and silence its demands.**

The promise of God, "I will not leave you as orphans," [21] is our reality. We have the loving care of a Father, who has met our every need.

He is "more than enough!"

Scriptures for Meditation:

(Romans 8:13) For if ye live after the flesh, ye shall die: but if ye through the Spirit do mortify the deeds of the body, ye shall live.

(Romans 7:24-25 *The Message*) I've tried everything and nothing helps. I'm at the end of my rope. Is there no one who can do anything for me? Isn't that the real question? The answer, thank God, is that Jesus Christ can and does. He acted to set things right in this life of contradictions where I want to serve God with all my heart and mind, but am pulled by the influence of sin to do something totally different.

---

[20] Ro 8:13 NKJV
[21] Jn 14:18 NASB

(Galatians 5:16-17) This I say then, Walk in the Spirit, and ye shall not fulfil the lust of the flesh. For the flesh lusteth against the Spirit, and the Spirit against the flesh: and these are contrary the one to the other: so that ye cannot do the things that ye would.

4

DAY AND NIGHT

This book of the law shall not depart out of thy mouth; but thou shalt meditate therein day and night, that thou mayest observe to do according to all that is written therein: for then thou shalt make thy way prosperous, and then thou shalt have good success (Joshua 1:8).

All my life, I have heard the saying, "People who talk to themselves are crazy." This proverb seems reasonable until we study the principles of God's Word on meditation. The Hebrew word translated "meditation" means to:

"murmur, ponder, mutter, speak, study, talk." [1]

This definition encourages us to reflect on God's Word, often in silence, AND to speak it to ourselves and to the

---

[1] H1897, *Strong's*

Lord. These actions deposit the Word of God into our spirit man. It increases knowledge, sharpens our perception, and lays the foundation for obedience.

The Word of God in Joshua 1:8 instructs us to meditate "day and night." Our continual meditation equips us to walk victoriously with the Lord.

In our home state of Florida, the stifling heat demands air-conditioning operate "day and night". Without it, we cannot work or relax. When, from time to time, an electrical problem turns the air-conditioning system off, it isn't long before every cell, muscle, tissue, and organ of our body begins to slow down. Shortly, all activity stops.

> *Meditation is as essential to our spirit as air-conditioning. Like gasoline in a car, meditation fills our lives with truth and propels us forward.*

Psalm 1 highlights the relationship between meditation and success. It warns us to avoid the counsel of sinners, the ungodly, and the scornful because their words of advice will not prepare us to follow the Word of God. **If we love our God, we will study His Word and embrace His commands, not the instructions of men.**

> *Through obedience to His commands, we prosper.*

Moses gave us a wonderful example of meditation and obedience when he commanded the people of God to "listen carefully" to God's voice. [2] The purpose of this heavenly counsel is clearly stated:

> *"to observe" God's commandments and "to do" them.* [3]

God promised them great benefits **if they would hear His words and heed His commands.**

The proverbs of Solomon state this same truth. They direct us to listen intently and look carefully at God's Word.[4] As we submit to the Word of God, the blessings of life and health abound.

These principles of meditation and obedience are defined in the New Testament by the apostle James.

Be doers of the word, and not hearers only. [5]

By hearing God's Word, we store the Scriptures in our spirit and our soul. This prepares our hearts to obey God's instructions. God, the Holy Spirit, will remind us of these many promises and orchestrate our work as "doers."

CHARACTERISTICS OF LOVE

The New Testament law of love is the leading

---

[2] Dt 28:1 MOF
[3] Dt 28:1,13
[4] Pr 4:20-22
[5] Jas 1:22 NKJV

challenge to the "doers" of God's Word.

The vast dimensions of this law instruct us to:

- Love the Lord your God. [6]
- Love one another. [7]
- Love your neighbor. [8]
- Love your brother. [9]
- Love your enemy. [10]
- Love all men. [11]

This law of love also instructs husbands to "love their wives" [12] and wives to "love their husbands." [13]

Without any doubt, **love is the continual command of God and the heart of the New Covenant.**

The most exhaustive description of God's love is found in 1 Corinthians 13. Here, we learn the different facets of God's love. God's love promotes longsuffering, kindness, good manners, and unselfishness. It rejects envy, pride, and anger.

Think of these many characteristics like the sections of an orange. As the sections of an orange unite to form one fruit, these elements combine to reveal the fullness of God's love.

---

[6] Mt 22:37;Mk 12:30;Lk 10:27
[7] Jn 13:34;Jn 15:12,17;Ro 13:8;2 Jn 1:5
[8] Mt 19:19;Mt 22:39;Mk 12:31;Gal 5:14;Jas 2:8
[9] 1Jn 2:10;1Jn 3:14;1Jn 4:21;1Pe 2:17
[10] Mt 5:44;Lk 6:27
[11] 1Th 3:12
[12] Eph 5:28,33
[13] Tit 2:4

MIX THE INGREDIENTS
OF LOVE

They blend together like the ingredients of a great cake. One of my favorite cake recipes, Sour Cream Pound Cake, has six essential ingredients. If any ingredient is omitted, the cake will fail.

In the same manner, every element and aspect of God's love must be manifested through our life to successfully fulfill God's commands.

For many years, my constant quest was to understand every characteristic of God's great love. My heart's desire was to:

---

love others as much as God loved me. [14]

Continually, I meditated on 1 Corinthians 13:4-8 and boldly confessed, "I am patient and kind. I am never envious, never boastful, and never jealous. I'm never selfish. I'm not easily provoked." I was determined to walk in His love.

With the help of the Holy Spirit, I studied the Scriptures that define God's love. This was long before we could print these Scriptures on a computer, so we painstakingly typed a list, using the many different translations of the Bible available to us at that time.

During one Florida beach vacation, I sat at the ocean's edge with one eye on my children and the other on my list of "love Scriptures." As I searched the Word of God, I asked Him to instruct me, forgive me, and perfect me in His love.

Truly, it seemed like an uphill battle. The love of God is SO big. But when we seek God with all our heart, He faithfully "guides us into truth." [15]

He works mightily in our spirit, soul, and body because he has chosen us "to live with Him and to be His holy and innocent and loving people." [16]

---

[14] Jn 13:34, author's paraphrase
[15] Jn 16:13, author's paraphrase
[16] Eph 1:4 CEV

I am so grateful. How can I thank Him? He is more than enough!

Scriptures for Meditation:

(Joshua 1:8) This book of the law shall not depart out of thy mouth; but thou shalt meditate therein day and night, that thou mayest observe to do according to all that is written therein: for then thou shalt make thy way prosperous, and then thou shalt have good success.

(Proverbs 4:20-22) My son, attend to my words; incline thine ear unto my sayings. Let them not depart from thine eyes; keep them in the midst of thine heart. For they are life unto those that find them, and health to all their flesh.

(John 16:13) Howbeit when he, the Spirit of truth, is come, he will guide you into all truth: for he shall not speak of himself; but whatsoever he shall hear, that shall he speak: and he will shew you things to come.

5

LOVE IS

Love is patient and kind. Love is not jealous, it does not brag, and it is not proud. Love is not rude, is not selfish, and does not get upset with others. Love does not count up wrongs that have been done. Love is not happy with evil but is happy with the truth. Love patiently accepts all things. It always trusts, always hopes, and always remains strong. Love never ends (1 Corinthians 13:4-8 NCV).

LOVE IS LONG-SUFFERING

This powerful passage in 1 Corinthians 13:4-8 begins, "Love suffers long." [1]

This is a ridiculous explanation, I suppose, but longsuffering is the opposite of "short-suffering." Short-suffering is displayed through our impatience, our quick angry words and reckless actions.

When love is longsuffering, it is:

---

[1] NKJV

- slow to lose patience [2]
- never tired of waiting [3]
- exhibits great restraint [4]

In other words, longsuffering love governs our actions and our words.

Vine's Complete Dictionary defines longsuffering as:

"that quality of self-restraint in the face of provocation which does not hastily retaliate or promptly punish; it is the opposite of anger, and is associated with mercy."

What a grand definition! Here, the words "anger" and "mercy" oppose each other.

Like two competitors in a boxing match, in the black trunks, representing the world, the flesh, and the devil, we see anger, provocation, hasty retaliation, and a desire for prompt punishment. In the white trunks, representing the Word of the living God, we have restraint and mercy. The desired winner is obvious.

The strongest example of longsuffering is God Himself.

Moses knew this well. After he had received the Ten

---

[2] *Phillips*
[3] BBE
[4] "Longsuffering," *Vine's*

Commandments, he descended Mount Sinai and found God's people worshipping a golden calf. Angrily, he dropped the stone tablets on which these commands were written, and they shattered.

Do you know what God did? Our loving Father gave His commandments a second time.

He said to Moses:

Cut two tablets of stone like the first ones, and I will write on these tablets the words that were on the first tablets which you broke. [5]

He was "merciful and gracious, longsuffering, and abundant in goodness and truth." [6]

The apostle Peter highlights God's longsuffering in 2 Peter 3:9. When challenged by scoffers, who questioned the reality of our Lord's second coming, he replied:

The Lord is...longsuffering toward us, not willing that any should perish but that all should come to repentance. [7]

The apostle Peter's inspired words bring us face-to-face with godly restraint and reveal **one of the greatest**

---

[5] Ex 34:1 NKJV
[6] Ex 34:6
[7] NKJV

manifestations of longsuffering—TIME.

When we are longsuffering, we give others time to seek God, time to repent, time to turn back, and time to change. Time is a gracious gift!

Our natural, fleshly temperament is the greatest obstacle of time and the overwhelming challenge of longsuffering and restraint.

If it dominates our lives, we pacify our flesh, appease our emotions, and excuse our behavior. We are not longsuffering. But when we believe that God is love and understand that His love dwells in us, we obey His command "to love our neighbor as ourselves." [8]

We yield to forbearance and endurance; [9] we are undisturbed and calm.[10]

It is God's will for every Christian to practice godly restraint, to imitate our heavenly Father, constantly walking the path of longsuffering with Him.

However, this cannot be accomplished by will power or through mental gymnastics. Instead, we trust the Word of God and the Spirit of God to enable us to be longsuffering. As we depend on them, we offer the wonderful gift of time to our family, to our friends, and also to those who declare themselves our enemy.

With God's help, longsuffering love continuously manifests in our lives.

---

[8] Mt 19:19, author's paraphrase
[9] "Longsuffering," *Webster's*, 1828
[10] "Patient," *Webster's*, 1959

GODLY RESTRAINT

LOVE IS KIND

Kindness is a close friend of longsuffering. First Corinthians 13:4 instructs us to be longsuffering AND kind. The conjunction "and" in this sentence is very significant. **We are not simply long-suffering. We are longsuffering AND kind.** These two powerful forces of love work together.

When we are kind, we are benevolent, helpful, and gracious. We respond to needs, building and improving the lives of others. The keen insight of *Noah Webster's First Edition of an American Dictionary of the English Language* defines kindness as:

> *"that temper or disposition which delights in contributing to the happiness of others, which is exercised cheerfully in gratifying their wishes, supplying their wants or alleviating their distresses."* [11]

This definition identifies the full nature of kindness.

A kind temperament always includes our words and actions.

If I said, "My neighbor is so kind to his wife," you would know he spoke lovingly to her and helped her with many tasks. His words and deeds reveal the kindness of his heart. I cannot say, "He is so kind," if he only speaks affectionately of her, but refuses to meet her needs.

The apostle Paul counseled husbands to love their wives as Christ loved the church. [12] Christ's love for the church commanded a sacrifice that was far more than a promise; it was an active reality. God's kindness was manifested "in word" and "in deed." [13]

Kindness in our homes also reveals itself through our conversation and our behavior. Our words and actions are

---

[11] "Kindness," *Webster's*, 1828
[12] Eph 5:25
[13] 1 Jn 3:18

partners laboring together to reflect the fullness of love.

God's love in every aspect of our lives is clearly defined by the instruction of Romans 12:21. It says:

Be not overcome of evil, but overcome evil with good.

What a significant word, "overcome."

When we overcome, we win. We prevail. We succeed. We are victorious. But how do we overcome?

We overcome when we refuse to respond unlovingly to evil deeds. Instead, we control our anger and answer antagonism with goodness.

Again, our words and our actions demonstrate the longsuffering and kindness of God.

I remember the first time a young lady in one of our classes understood God's principle to overcome evil with good. She was having a difficult time with a co-worker. In fact, they had become enemies, but the truth of God's Word convinced her she must demonstrate His love.

One day, we were discussing different godly love-inspired actions she could make to win this co-worker's heart when this young lady's countenance fell.

"What is it?" I asked, concerned.

"Oh," she replied, "I was just thinking about everything I must do for her."

Any demonstration of kindness for someone so

"unlovely" seemed overwhelming. Though the love of God propelled her to action, her body and soul staggered in objection.

Now, this is very important! Here is the answer to our friend's distress:

Kindness is not dictated by our feelings. It is a command of the Word of God. It is a choice. Therefore, we choose to respond to God's Word without the approval of our emotions.

From time to time, everyone struggles to restrain their emotions and allow the love of God to dominate their life. I remember one such occasion in my life. Intent on apologizing to a friend, I paced endlessly by my telephone.

I said to myself, "I can do this. I must do this."

Yet I hesitated to act. Finally, in desperation I cried out, "Holy Spirit, help me! Love of God on the inside, Greater One, rise up big within me!"

Thank God, His love is in our spirit.

When we decide to obey this love, the Holy Spirit strengthens us.

With His help, I overcame my fears and successfully made the phone call.

Many people never fully understand how to respond to difficult situations with God's love, His long-suffering, and His kindness. **But, we must know, when we yield to our feelings, we forfeit the ability of God's Word and His Spirit to aid us.**

Some time ago, a friend narrowly avoided a car accident. The incident was not his fault, yet the offending driver lashed out at him, rude and irate. With genuine concern our friend asked, "Can I take you to a gas station? Is there anything you need?" He refused to speak emotional words.

Others might have said, "You should have stayed on your side of the road! You could have killed me!"

However, our friend allowed God's love to rule him.

Someone who knows him well told me, "He's always patient." What a compliment! What a great example of longsuffering and kindness!

Like my friend, **every Christian must bear trauma without wrath and anger**. We must refuse to act on "ungodly thoughts" or "render evil for evil." [14] Instead, our behavior should be benevolent and helpful, forbearing and restrained. This is God's way, and we honor Him when this is our way, too.

LOVE IS SEEMLY

A necessary addition to the life of every Christian is found in 1 Corinthians 13:5, "Love doth not behave itself unseemly."

The word "unseemly" is seldom used in modern vocabulary, so we must ask ourselves, "What is unseemly behavior?"

Or in reverse, "What is seemly behavior?"

The answer to this question is easily discerned through different Bible translations.

---

[14] 1 Th 5:15

The New Testament in Modern English by J.B. Phillips states:

Love has good manners.

In the *World English Bible,* we read that love:

---

doesn't behave itself inappropriately.

Still further perception is added when the *Wuest* translation states:

Love ... does not act unbecomingly.

My, I love Bible translations. Through these learned scholars, the Holy Spirit enlarges our vision.

Another scholar whose wisdom aids our vision is Noah Webster. In *Webster's New Collegiate Dictionary,* the word "seemly" means:

"suited to the occasion, purpose, or one's character or position"

It also means:

"fitting or proper in respect to the conventional standards of good form or taste."

At first glance, these definitions seem far afield from the work of our Bible scholars. Yet they are complimentary and graphically increase our understanding.

If we consider Noah Webster's definition, "suited to one's position," we ask: What *is* our position as a Christian?

The answer is obvious. When we accepted Jesus as our Savior and Lord, we became children of God.

The apostle John announced this grand truth.

But as many as received Him, to them gave He power to become the sons of God, even to them that believe on His name.[15]

He amplifies this declaration in 1 John 3:2 with the word "now."

*Beloved, **now** are we the sons of God.*

These Scriptures define our position. We are children

---

[15] Jn 1:12

of God; we are sons of God, NOW.

With this understanding, we ask two other important questions:

- Is there a standard of behavior for the sons of God?
- How can the sons of God achieve this standard?

The answer to these questions is revealed in one verse of Scripture.

Be ye therefore followers of God, as dear children. [16]

Obviously, **God is the pattern and standard for our conduct.** When we follow Him, our behavior will be fitting, proper, and in good form. It will be seemly.

The attitudes and actions of God, our Father, are exhibited in the life of Jesus. He showed us exactly what God is like. [17] Jesus reminded us of this truth when He said:

He that hath seen me hath seen the Father. [18]

---

[16] Eph 5:1
[17] Heb 1:3 NCV
[18] Jn 14:9

Through His life, we can follow God and come face-to-face with seemly behavior. Isn't this the goal presented to us by our Bible scholars? They taught us that love has good manners, acts becomingly, and behaves appropriately.

We can only achieve this standard by imitating God, our Father, and Jesus Christ, our Lord.

As we imitate Jesus, our behavior, like His, represents God "in every way" [19] and our conduct is seemly.

LOVE IS UNSELFISH

As representatives of God, there is no question that we follow God's instruction in 1 Corinthians 13:5, "[Love] seeketh not her own." Every Christian understands this command.

Yet frequently, the voice of selfishness blazes, "You give me that! You listen to me! You better do what I said!"

With great authority, selfishness demands those things that bring personal comfort and gain. It chooses the biggest piece of pie, the most comfortable chair, the best vacation time, and the first place in line.

Selfishness is relentless and inconsiderate.

Selfishness is not concerned about the needs and desires of others. It constantly cries, "Do this for me. Fix this for me. Bring that to me." Me! Me! Me! It demands its way and insists on its own rights.

---

[19] Heb 1:3 CEV

LOVE IS UNSELFISH

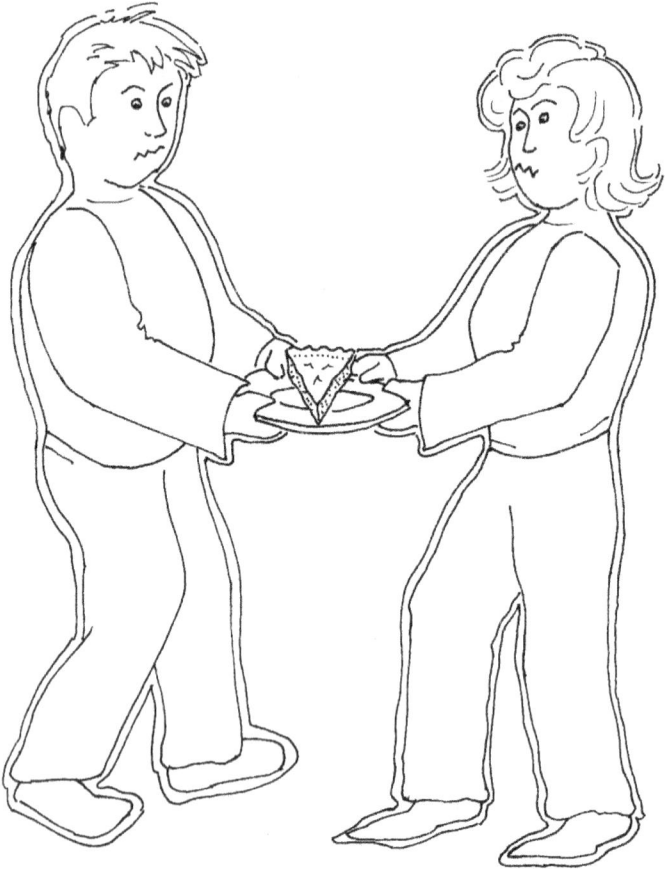

But we, the sons of God, are not self-seeking. When God's unselfish love guides our lives, it gives you the best piece of pie. It alters vacation plans for your benefit. It chooses the last place in line, insisting you stand in first place.

The apostle Paul helps us understand unselfish love by reminding us:

Let each esteem others better than himself. [20]

In this verse, "each" is an important word. EACH of us must obey the Word of God and unselfishly consider our neighbor's need. *The New American Standard Bible* emphasizes this.

Do not merely look out for your own personal interests.

Years ago, this was my goal. I decided to practice this principle of God and always put my husband's desire first. I would be completely unselfish.

After concentrating on unselfishness for only a short time, I was totally overcome. It was too hard. In despair, I bowed my head and cried out to God, "I can't do it!"

I will never forget the response. Quietly, my spirit said, "You have no choice."

That's it! "You have no choice."

Now, before you respond in disbelief, I must tell you these words saved my life. The will of God had been decisively declared and **selfishness was NOT an option.** I

---

[20] Php 2:3, NKJV

would obey God's command. "I would do all things as Christ strengthened me." [21]

From that day forward, God's command, "Love is never selfish," [22] was not as hard or difficult as before. The Lord was my helper. I had decided!

Scriptures for Meditation:

(Romans 12:10) Be kindly affectioned one to another with brotherly love; in honour preferring one another.

(Ephesians 5:1-2) Be ye therefore followers of God, as dear children. And walk in love, as Christ also hath loved us, and hath given himself for us an offering and a sacrifice to God for a sweetsmelling savour.

(1 Thessalonians 5:15) See that none render evil for evil unto any man; but ever follow that which is good, both among yourselves, and to all men.

(1 John 3:18) My little children, let us not love in word, neither in tongue; but in deed and in truth.

---

[21] Php 4:13, author's paraphrase
[22] 1Co 13:5 MOF

6

WE CAN BE CHANGED

But we all, with open face beholding as in a glass the glory of the Lord, are changed into the same image from glory to glory, even as by the Spirit of the Lord (2 Corinthians 3:18).

LOVE WILL NOT ENVY

God's way of love declares, "Love does not envy." [1] I love the definition of envy from *Webster's New Collegiate Dictionary*:

"chagrin or discontent at the excellence or good fortune of another."

This unveils the attitude of envy. Envy is dissatisfied when you purchase a new car, while I continue to drive an older model. It responds angrily if your child succeeds in school as my child struggles. It covets your position, resents your promotion, and speaks disparagingly of your ability.

---

[1] 1 Co 13:4, NKJV

ENVY IS AN ENEMY

Envy is a determined enemy.

There are several powerful examples of envy in the Scriptures. In Genesis 26:14, we read:

For he [Isaac] had possession of flocks, and possession of herds, and great store of servants: and the Philistines envied him.

Indeed, in the land of the Philistines Isaac was "very great". [2] King Abimelech, the leader of the Philistines, saw that the Lord was with Isaac and confessed:

Thou art now the blessed of the Lord. [3]

Another example of envy is found in the life of Joseph. Every student of the Bible is familiar with the story of Joseph and his coat of many colors. Joseph's father "loved Joseph more than all his children" [4] and made him a special coat.

Because of this, Joseph's brothers hated him. Their resentment deepened after Joseph related two dreams in which his family bowed down to him.

The *New King James Version* graphically records:

And his brothers envied him. [5]

[2] Ge 26:13
[3] Ge 26:29
[4] Ge 37:3
[5] Ge 37:11, NKJV

Their envy caused them to plot his death. [6] Envy, strife, and hatred are dangerous enemies of God's love.

James 3:16 states:

For where envy and strife is, there is confusion and every evil work.

Did you notice the word "every?" **Envy opens the door to EVERY evil work.**

In the New Testament, the envy of the chief priests plotted the death of our Lord. Resentment against Paul and Barnabas brought blasphemous attacks on their lives. Throughout the Bible, envy produced hatred and many deadly schemes.

Envy is truly a dangerous enemy.

LOVE WILL NOT BOAST

We find another enemy of our soul in 1 Corinthians 13:4, "[Love] vaunteth not itself."

This word "vaunteth" puzzles us.

When it is united with the phrase that follows, we become more perplexed.

[Love] vaunteth not itself, and is not puffed up

---

[6] Ge 37:11

Without a scriptural understanding of these uncommon words, we cannot comprehend this loving command of God.

One of the best ways to clarify the meaning of these phrases is to study them from several Bible translations.

Other texts read:

- It does not boast. [7]
- Love ... doesn't strut, doesn't have a swelled head. [8]
- Love has no high opinion of itself. [9]
- It is not conceited. [10]

These scholarly translations enable us to understand God's command.

God's *love* never promotes itself. It does not cry, "Look at me!" *It* never exalts or flatters itself.

People who advertise their own importance are often self-possessed and "pushy." You don't have to insist they undertake a job that causes them to be noticed. Instead, you must urge them to delegate responsibilities to others. Without hesitation, they shove their way to the front, run over anyone in their path, and seat themselves in first place. They lack respect for the needs and desires of others.

The instructions of the Holy Spirit through the apostle Paul help us reject this ungodly pride.

---

[7] NIV
[8] *Message*
[9] BBE
[10] AMP

His exhortation warns us:

Let nothing be done through selfish ambition or conceit, but in lowliness of mind let each esteem others better than himself. [11]

This powerful verse teaches that we must not, indeed we cannot, magnify ourselves. We must first value others. The apostle Paul writing to the church at Rome confirms this truth.

Love each other as brothers and sisters and honor others more than you do yourself. [12]

This aspect of God's command of love cannot be overstated. We know, "God so loved the world," [13] that He sacrificed His Son. If we love God, we will also sacrifice our lives for others. We will "do unto others" [14] before we consider our own need.

I love the words of Jesus:

---

[11] Php 2:3, NKJV
[12] Ro 12:10 CEV
[13] Jn 3:16
[14] Mt 7:12, author's paraphrase

And whosoever will be chief among you, let him be your servant. [15]

He honored these words when He washed the disciples' feet. His example inspires us to serve others.

WE CHOOSE

"ME FIRST"

"SERVE OTHERS"

[15] Mt 20:27

Each of us must choose between "do unto others" and the constant clamor of our pride. The pendulum swings to the left and right awaiting our choice. Do we work for God and serve others? Or do we value ourselves above all else?

The command of the Scripture is clear. We must decide!

By love serve one another." [16]

LOVE WILL NOT RESPOND ANGRILY

Every Christian should be acutely aware of God's command, "[Love] is not easily provoked." [17] My, stop and ponder that for a few minutes. What an expressive word, "provoked!"

When we are "provoked," we are exasperated, irritated, and often enraged.

We respond angrily to a person or situation shouting, "You make me so mad! You can't do that to me! Who do you think you are!" Stirred to anger and emotionally triggered by our circumstances, we react.

If you are married, I know you understand this. A husband comes home from work after a long day. Because his wife had a tiring and disruptive day, she yields to her

[16] Gal 5:13
[17] 1 Co 13:5

flesh and snaps at him. In exasperation, he angrily responds to her words. Of course, this drama could be reversed. The husband could be the first to provoke and upend the behavior of his wife.

So often, we allow the anger of others to dictate our behavior. If they "holler and carry on," we join them. If they "spit on us," we "spit on them." **But when we follow our Lord's example, we refuse to reciprocate.**

In 1 Peter 2:23 we read:

He [Jesus] did not retaliate when He was insulted. When He suffered, He did not threaten to get even. He left His case in the hands of God, who always judges fairly. [18]

What powerful words! **One way to triumph when we want to retaliate is to postpone our response.** By delaying our reply, we prevent harsh, unkind, and malicious words.

The directive of the Holy Spirit from the apostle James confirms this principle. He exhorted us to:

---

be swift to hear, slow to speak, slow to wrath. [19]

We can follow his exhortation if we respond, "I can't discuss that now."

---

[18] NLT
[19] Jas 1:19

In our early years of marriage, I was always the first to be irritated and respond angrily. If there was any disagreement, my husband, Wayne, would "pout" and I would "shout." Even when I was wrong, I could win the argument because I would not surrender. I simply asserted my opinion through loud words until I prevailed.

To control my flesh and restrain my anger, I turned to the Scripture for help. I found my answer in Proverbs 15:1. It states:

A soft answer turneth away wrath: but grievous words stir up anger.

The word "soft" in this verse is translated by Bible scholars as:

- gentle [20]
- pleasant [21]
- kind [22]
- mild [23]

In *Webster's New Collegiate Dictionary*, "soft" is defined:

---

[20] *Message*
[21] BER
[22] CEV
[23] MOF

"devoid of all roughness, harshness, or intensity."

These definitions led me to speak very quietly and whisper when I became angry. This may seem foolish, but it worked well for me.

It has been many years since anger prompted me to lower my voice to a whisper. However recently, in a business situation I was "exceedingly provoked." To my surprise, I leaned across the counter and explained my disagreement in soft tones.

I laughed at myself afterward, but the situation was soon resolved. Thank God, the Word is always true! "A soft answer turns away wrath."

People make so many excuses for their unloving behavior. They say:

- "I was under great pressure."
- "I didn't feel well."
- "I just couldn't take it anymore."
- "You just don't understand."

But believe me, I do understand. For many years I meditated day and night on God's command of love to overcome the domination of my flesh.

I am so grateful that the Holy Spirit helps us. He works mightily in us, enabling us to obey God's loving decree.

There is, however, one truth we cannot reject.

We must desire to change.

We can no longer pacify our flesh crying, "You know how I am." We must lay aside fleshly determination and follow our Lord's example. **If our heart is fully surrendered to Him, then the Holy Spirit will teach us and change us.** God has promised!

His Word proclaims:

We all, with open face beholding as in a glass the glory of the Lord, are changed into the same image from glory to glory, even as by the Spirit of the Lord. [24]

Truly, we can be changed! We can walk in God's love!

Scriptures for Meditation:

(Proverbs 15:1) A soft answer turneth away wrath: but grievous words stir up anger.

(Galatians 5:13) For, brethren, ye have been called unto liberty; only use not liberty for an occasion to the flesh, but by love serve one another.

(Philippians 2:3) Let nothing be done through strife or vainglory; but in lowliness of mind let each esteem other better than themselves.

---

[24] 2 Co 3:16

(James 1:19) Wherefore, my beloved brethren, let every man be swift to hear, slow to speak, slow to wrath.

(James 3:16) For where envying and strife is, there is confusion and every evil work.

7

I'M MAD!

And be ye kind one to another, tenderhearted, forgiving one another, even as God for Christ's sake hath forgiven you (Ephesians 4: 32).

Have you ever been so angry that you wanted to get even? Was your thinking controlled by fleshly demands? Did you decide to never speak to the offender again?

I imagine all of us have been tempted by these ungodly emotional responses. Angry and irritated, we extend judgment and dictate punishment, instead of honoring the goodness and forgiveness of God. Oh, how very wrong we are!

At times like these, we appoint ourselves as judge and jury. We declare the offending person "guilty," and without deliberation, rebuke them and expose their error. We replay and reconstruct our contention, launching every word like a missile. Finally, we lapse into silence, but our eyes continue to emit daggers of agony and our heart murmurs in complaint.

What can we do in this situation and what should we do? Is there an answer that repairs the damage of anger and strife? Without any doubt the answer is found in the

Scriptures. **It is captured in one word, "forgive."**

In the gospel of Mark, Jesus said:

_____

Forgive, if you have anything against anyone. [1]

_____

Again, in the writings of Luke we read:

_____

[1] Mk 11:25 NASB

Forgive, and ye shall be forgiven. [2]

We also hear these instructions in the Lord 's Prayer. Jesus said:

And forgive us our debts, as we forgive our debtors. [3]

Forgiveness is a characteristic of God's love. **It is a decision to release a person from responsibility or guilt.**

When we forgive, we refuse to retaliate.

In *Webster's New Collegiate Dictionary*, "forgive" is defined as:

"to give up resentment or claim to requital on account of (an offense)." [4]

This definition seems overwhelming, especially if I'm mad. But here is good news! **Forgiveness does not depend on our will power or on bulldog tenacity.** It is not an emotional response dictated by our feelings.

Forgiveness is a decision to follow God's command to "love one another." [5] It springs from God's supernatural

---

[2] Lk 6:37
[3] Mt 6:12
[4] *Webster's*, 1959
[5] Jn 13:34, NIV

love which was poured into our spirit when we were born again.

This godly forgiveness subdues the hatred and malice demanded by our flesh. Our flesh desires revenge and promotes retaliation. It accents, underlines, and highlights hostilities.

Rebelliously, it shouts, "I tell you what! I don't have to take that!" Blazing in anger and smoldering in resentment, it marches against God's declaration to:

forgive if you have ought against any. [6]

I remember an incident in my life that elevated the demands of my flesh to new heights. I am so glad the Word of God rescued me. Through the pen of the Apostle Paul, the Holy Spirit proclaims:

"Be angry, and do not sin": do not let the sun go down on your wrath. [7]

At first, I embraced this verse as an excuse to continue pouting. My anger began after sundown, so I told myself, "I can deal with this tomorrow." I interpreted the Scripture to accommodate my anger.

In my spirit, I knew this verse meant I must forgive

quickly. **If we hold a grudge, we protect the offense and allow anger to dominate us.** Our emotions bitterly demand to be vindicated, while our thoughts drive us further and further away from God's gracious forgiveness.

But we cannot permit our flesh and emotions to pressure us and lead us astray. We must obey the instructions of God's Word.

In 1 Corinthians 13:5 the *King James Version* of God's Word says:

[Love] thinketh no evil. [8]

The Amplified Bible expands this thought when it says:

Love...takes no account of the evil done to it [it pays no attention to a suffered wrong].

A third scholar asserts:

[Love] does not compile statistics of evil. [9]

These translations highlight our propensity to meditate

---

[8] 1 Co 13:5

[9] Phillips, J.B., *Letters To Young Churches*, (New York: The MacMillan Company, 1953), 61

on and carefully record offenses. They remind us that we cannot heed the voice of retaliation that frequently cries, "That's the third time she has done that to me. If she does that one more time, I will ..."

My! My! My! **God's love "does not brood over an injury."** [10] Instead of moodily or anxiously rehearsing the drama of an offense, we acknowledge the promises of Gods' Word. We confess ungodly thoughts and abort any evil intentions. We do not retaliate!

FORGIVE

The Holy Spirit opens our understanding and helps us embrace these instructions from God's Word. Because He works mightily in our spirit, we are undisturbed by harsh words.

When we are accused, we do not mumble, complain, or broadcast our dissatisfaction. Instead, we offer to others the kindness and forgiveness of God. The love of God in us:

does not hold grudges and will hardly even notice when others do it wrong. [11]

Kindness and forgiveness are partners. We see this in Ephesians 4:32 when it proclaims:

---

[10] 1 Co 13:5, *Knox*
[11] 1Co 13:5 *Living*

And be kind to one another, tenderhearted, forgiving one another, even as God in Christ forgave you. [12]

Here, a tender, compassionate heart speaks with great kindness and quickly forgives. Yet the true magnitude of this forgiveness unfolds in the final words:

forgiving one another, even as God in Christ forgave you.

What a declaration! We are kind to others, and we forgive others as God has forgiven us! This is emphasized when *The Message Bible* says:

Forgive one another as quickly and thoroughly as God in Christ forgave you.

Did you notice the word "thoroughly?" **God's forgiveness is thorough. It is not half-hearted, occasional, partial, or biased.**

In fact, according to the psalmist, its boundaries stretch "as far as the east is from the west." [13] I love this

---

analogy because east and west never meet. If our sins are separated by this distance, they are completely removed.

Our knowledge of God's complete forgiveness is further enhanced when God declares:

I, even I, am He who blots out your transgressions for My own sake; and I will not remember your sins. [14]

An object that is blotted out can no longer be seen. It is gone or removed.

The prophet Micah adds to this truth saying:

God casts all our sins into the depths of the sea. [15]

If our sins are in the deepest sea, they are concealed. This phenomenal revelation unveils the Father's heart. **He blots out our sin for His "own sake."**

As a parent, I understand this astounding statement. We bless our children because our heart overflows in love for them. We give generously because without a tangible expression of love our heart isn't satisfied.

God's gracious forgiveness is evidence of His bountiful love for His children, but we must acknowledge our sin and ask for forgiveness. As we confess our sin, our merciful

---

[14] Isa 43:25 NKJV
[15] Mic 7:19, author's paraphrase

Father forgives us. We see this marvelous fact proclaimed in 1 John 1:9.

If we confess our sins, he is faithful and just to forgive us our sins, and to cleanse us from all unrighteousness.

This verse always stands out in my mind because of the word "all." If a Christian confesses his sin, God cleanses him from ALL iniquity. We cannot enjoy fellowship with God if we do not confess our sins. We must repent and allow the blood of Jesus to cleanse us.

The hymnist, Robert Lowry, penned this glorious truth in words frequently sung.

"What can wash away my sin?
Nothing but the blood of Jesus
What can make me whole again?
Nothing but the blood of Jesus." [16]

Through Jesus' blood, we are instantly forgiven and again, in fellowship with God.

---

[16] "Nothing But The Blood," Words & Music: Robert Lowry, in *Gospel Music*, by William Doane and Robert Lowry (New York: Biglow & Main, 1876),
<http://www.cyberhymnal.org/htm/n/b/nbtblood.htm>, Accessed 17 May 2011.

AND FORGET

God's forgiveness of all our sin and our fellowship with Him encourage us to forgive others. The command of the Scripture is to forgive them "seventy times seven," [17] or 490 times a day. This must include those we deem wonderful and those we think are vile and offensive.

Jesus said to forgive:

---

if you have anything against anyone. [18]

This principle is very difficult when people insult or threaten us. At those moments, our flesh wants to publicize the offense. The last words we want to hear are "forgive, as you have been forgiven." [19]

But if we imitate God, we will not allow offenses to rule us.

We cannot board up our heart and hold God's forgiveness captive while the fleshly desire for retaliation dominates our behavior. We must thoroughly, purposefully, refuse the memory of sin and offense.

This challenge to forgive and forget reminds me of a grandmother who frequently hid her money and other precious belongings. Usually, she couldn't locate them again, so her family decided to hide them for her.

---

[17] Mt 18:21-22
[18] Mk 11:25 NASB
[19] Eph 4:32, author's paraphrase

LOVE COVERS SIN

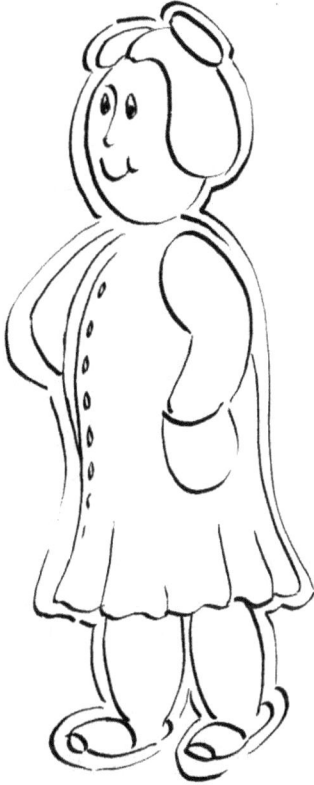

On one particular occasion, a sum of money was hidden in a housecoat pocket. Later, when she could not find the money, her family reminded her to look in her pocket. However, the pocket was empty. Without their knowledge, she had moved the money. In fact, the money was never recovered.

In like manner, **our loving God hides our sins, and they**

are never recovered. He does not expose confessed sin or rehearse past offenses.

Can you imagine the anguish if God publicized our sins? Our soul would be tortured if God said, "I thought I would forget your sin, but I can't."

Oh, the wonder of His forgiveness! With great joy, we hear Him say:

I will be merciful to their unrighteousness, and their sins and their iniquities will I remember no more. [20]

As Christians, we follow God's example.

In trying situations, we do not respond angrily or harbor resentment. Instead, we honor the loving forgiveness of God and choose to forget the offense.

Not guided by our feelings, we imitate God. The Word of God addresses this in Ephesians 5:1.

Be imitators of God, therefore, as dearly loved children and live a life of love. [21]

In the business world, a new employee carefully follows the instructions of his trainer until he is proficient at his new job. **Similarly, we dedicate ourselves to God's**

---

[20] Heb 8:12
[21] NIV

instructions of love and forgiveness. Like Him, we forgive and forget quickly.

This is not easy if we do not feel responsible. On one occasion, I was certain I was not guilty. A friend had asked me for counsel regarding the sale or transfer of some property. As we talked, she listed three possible courses of action. But I noticed a fourth option she had seemingly overlooked. Without telling her what to do, I mentioned this additional plan should also be considered. Instantly, she became offended, and for several weeks, she refused to speak to me.

Over time, the Holy Spirit began to deal with me to telephone her and apologize. I was defiant. I said, "I'm not going to do it. I didn't do anything wrong. She can just call me."

Oh dear! Did you know this is not correct? **We are often under the false impression that the one responsible for the mistake instigates the apology.** But it is the person who is spiritually mature, who knows something must be done, who speaks first.

The Scripture says:

Brethren, if a man be overtaken in a fault, ye which are spiritual, restore such an one in the spirit of meekness; considering thyself, lest thou also be tempted. [22]

This powerful truth on reconciliation must always

[22] Gal 6:1

guide our actions.

Here, then, was my choice. I could allow my flesh to control my actions, or I could yield to the instruction of God.

The inspired words of the Apostle Paul note:

For the flesh lusts against the Spirit, and the Spirit against the flesh; and these are contrary to one another, so that you do not do the things that you wish. [23]

He also declared, "Walk in the Spirit, and you shall not fulfill the lust of the flesh." [24]

Thank God, for the counsel of His Word. When His Word dominates our lives, we will crucify our flesh and heed the voice of the Holy Spirit. He guides our spirit in the ways of God.

Well, one day, I tired of the debate between my spirit and my flesh. I called her and said, "You know I love you. I wouldn't want there to be any hard feelings between us."

She began to cry. She said, "It's my fault."

I had to bite my tongue. I wanted to say, "I knew that all the time." But I didn't.

We must follow the Word of God and be guided by its precepts. It says:

---

[23] Gal 5:17 NKJV
[24] Gal 5:16 NKJV

If it be possible, as much as lieth in you, live peaceably with all men. [25]

I didn't hear any voices that day, but I did sense the approval of our God. I had followed His Word even though my flesh rebelled.

Before, when my flesh was not submitted to God's Word, I wanted to hear God say, "I know it's not your fault. I know you tried. Just relax. If she doesn't call you and apologize, don't worry about it." But after I apologized, the peace of God flooded my heart and confirmed God's Word.

Each of us must quickly seek reconciliation and forgiveness. Immediately, with heartfelt repentance, we respond to God's love. This is the command of heaven. It is the godly principle that guides our behavior as children of God. With God's strength, we forgive and forget.

Scriptures for Meditation:

(Matthew 18:21-22) Then came Peter to him, and said, Lord, how oft shall my brother sin against me, and I forgive him? till seven times? Jesus saith unto him, I say not unto thee, Until seven times: but, Until seventy times seven.

(Mark 11:25) And when ye stand praying, forgive, if ye have ought against any: that your Father also which is in heaven may forgive you your trespasses.

---

[25] Ro 12:18

(Ephesians 4:26) Be ye angry, and sin not: let not the sun go down upon your wrath.

(Ephesians 4:32) And be ye kind one to another, tenderhearted, forgiving one another, even as God for Christ's sake hath forgiven you.

8

DO UNTO OTHERS

And as ye would that men should do to you, do ye also to them likewise (Luke 6:31).

Every Christian has the supernatural ability to love others. These loving actions are orchestrated by God's divine love.

In the Greek language, God's love is the word *agape*. **God's *agape* love refers to a decision, not a feeling or emotion.** It contrasts with the Greek word, *phileo*, which means:

"to be a friend to (fond of [an individual or an object]), i.e. have affection for (denoting personal attachment, as a matter of sentiment or feeling." [1]

Although we cherish warm, sentimental moments and affectionate friendships, **God's powerful love steps beyond emotional attachments and is guided by His Word.**

God's *agape* love rejects the operation of our mind and

---

[1] G5368, *Strong's*

emotions when they do not agree with the Word of God. **We cannot adequately represent God's love if our mind is not saturated with His thoughts.** But through meditation in the Scriptures, our mind is renewed, and our thoughts come into agreement with God. Then, instead of OUR way, we embrace GOD's way, and every step we take yields to His love.

Without hesitation, we devote ourselves to others, surrendering our time, talent, and finances to meet their needs. We become more than willing to represent God's *agape* love.

OUR WORDS AND ACTIONS

Frequently, our commitment to help others is time-consuming and inconvenient. As we leave our house on a very important errand, a friend's need might delay us. Later, while we are resting, a phone call disturbs us. While we are praying and enjoying the presence of God, a neighbor asks for assistance with his car. At the most inopportune moments, our friends reach out to us with sometimes desperate needs.

With great emotion, they say, "I am so sick," or, "I just needed someone to talk to." They might say, "My kids are driving me crazy," or, "My husband doesn't love me anymore." There are so many possible times of distress.

But this agape love in our spirit is the servant of God's will. It shares His heart and works diligently as His vessel on earth. It responds continually to the call of Jesus:

Do for others what you would like them to do for you. [2]

It cherishes His words, words like:

- Do good.
- Be merciful.
- Give.
- Bless. [3]

God's love carefully follows scriptural exhortations to:

- Be courteous.
- Seek peace. [4]

This is the job of love, and it is our job as God's children.

Every Christian is a "doer!" The book of James declares this fact. It says:

But be ye doers of the word, and not hearers only, deceiving your own selves. [5]

---

[2] Mt. 7:12 NLT
[3] Lk 6:35-36,38;Mt 5:44
[4] 1Pe 3:8,11
[5] Jas 1:22

Deception is an ungodly foe. When a man is deceived, he is certain that he is holding fast to the truth. He does not realize his error. If we are NOT doers of God's love, we are deceived! **Our words and our actions should communicate God's love.**

This response of word and deed is encouraged by many New Testament authors. The apostle Paul declares:

Whatever you SAY or DO should be done in the name of the Lord Jesus. [6]

James further guides us when he speaks disparagingly of those who say, "Be warmed and filled," [7] yet refuse to meet the need.

The love of God cannot be represented by words without action. **We must speak lovingly AND work diligently.**

Furthermore, God's love assists others without anger or bitterness. It does not murmur and complain,[8] but communicates encouragement and blessing. It observes needs and is actively involved in solving problems.

The love of God is always merciful, kind, and confidential. How is this possible? God is in us! He is the Greater One [9] and we are His temple! [10] When we call upon

---

[6] Col 3:17 CEV
[7] Jas 2:16 NKJV
[8] Php 2:14
[9] 1Jn 4:4
[10] 1Co3:16;1Co 6:19

Him, [11] He leads us by His Spirit. [12]

The Spirit of God helps us understand God's will and empowers us to lovingly support those who need His care. We are dependent on the Holy Spirit! With His help, we will be DOERS of God's work.

OUR OBEDIENCE

It is much easier to follow God's instructions to DO UNTO OTHERS when relationships are loving and kind. It is harder when difficult people constantly press us for support.

Usually, we want to loudly proclaim, "No, I can't help you," while muttering to ourselves, "And that's final."

Yet God's scriptural directive is to:

---

overcome evil with good. [13]

This instruction goes far beyond giving words of love and offering forgiveness. It surpasses loving thoughts and honest intentions. **We must also DO GOOD.**

Oh, sometimes our mind rejects loving action, choosing instead to shout, complain, and gossip. But this is not God's way. We must love others unconditionally.

Whenever I teach overcoming evil with good, I ask the students, "What good thing are you going to do today for

---

[11] Jas 4:8
[12] Ro 8:14
[13] Ro 12:21

that irritating person in your life?" The students are often startled by this question. In spite of God's instructions, they had not thought to DO anything.

DO
UNTO OTHERS

I usually suggest buying coffee or donuts, sending flowers, or writing a gracious note. It's a little trite to say it this way, I guess, but, **"DO is something you DO."**

Years ago, someone came to me about a distressing relationship with a family member. When I suggested she send flowers to this relative, she was hesitant. She didn't understand God's Word about loving actions. Yet a week or so later, she sent a bouquet of flowers and bridged the chasm that had developed between them. In that moment, she overcame!

Another testimony of success was shared with me by a friend. She had a serious breach with her neighbor, and they had not spoken for a very long time. One night while fixing a casserole for supper, she was impressed by the Lord to also prepare one for her neighbor. Initially, she made excuses to the Lord. She told Him that it was too late in the day; she was sure her neighbor had already started supper.

When this did not pacify her heart, she argued that it was a very spicy casserole, and they probably wouldn't eat it. Eventually, she obeyed the urging of her spirit. Together, they wept and were reconciled.

When the Scripture instructs us to "overcome evil with good," it declares:

Therefore if thine enemy hunger, feed him; if he thirst, give him drink: for in so doing thou shalt heap coals of fire on his head. [14]

Now, I am certain if someone poured hot coals on your head, you would notice. This action would make a difference. I believe this is the intent of these words inspired by the Holy Spirit. Several scholars agree.

The *Jamieson, Fausset, and Brown Commentary* proclaims:

---

[14] Ro 12:20

"As metals are melted by heaping coals upon them, so is the heart softened by kindness."

Albert Barnes' Notes on the Bible writes:

"The apostle is speaking of the natural effect or result of showing [one] kindness."

Additionally, the songwriter penned, "They will know we are Christians by our love." [15]

But does loving action always succeed? Yes, it always works IN YOU. Of course, there will be people who ignore your kind, generous gestures. No matter what their response, **if we "do unto others" with God's love, we are rewarded.**

Our responsibility is to love the offender, to bless them, pray for them, and DO GOOD unto them. The words of Jesus gave this command. He said:

But I say unto you, Love your enemies, bless them that curse you, DO GOOD to them that hate you,

---

[15] "They'll Know We Are Christians By Our Love" Words and Music: Peter Scholtes, Additional Words and Music: Carolyn Arends, © 1966 by F.E.L. Publications, Ltd./ASCAP (1925 Pontius Avenue, Los Angeles, CA 90025), <http://www.carolynarends.com/music/lyrics/tkwac.html>, Accessed 17 May 2011.

and pray for them which despitefully use you, and
persecute you. [16]

If this Scripture is in our heart, we refuse to retaliate.

It is interesting to note that *Webster's New Collegiate Dictionary* defines "retaliate" as:

"to return evil for evil."

The *New Century Version* of Romans 12:17 agrees. It says:

If someone does wrong to you, do not pay him back by doing wrong to him.

We see this again in the Psalms. The psalmist testifies:

Fret not thyself in any wise to do evil. [17]

These instructions are very clear. The route of victory does not include evil.

Even so, it is very difficult to DO GOOD when we have

---

[16] Mt 5:44
[17] Ps 37:8

been insulted or injured. But we choose to:

---

let God, the One who judges rightly, take care of [us]. [18]

He will do what is right! In fact, He is the only one who can do what is right! **Our judgment, based on our feelings, emotions, and reasoning, is faulty.** However, if we yield to God's judgment, He can extend mercy, orchestrate reconciliation, and judge fairly.

And isn't that the point? Doesn't *agape* love give everyone an opportunity to change? I think so! I think so!

Scriptures for Meditation:

(Matthew 5:44) But I say unto you, Love your enemies, bless them that curse you, do good to them that hate you, and pray for them which despitefully use you, and persecute you.

(Luke 6:35) But love ye your enemies, and do good, and lend, hoping for nothing again; and your reward shall be great, and ye shall be the children of the Highest: for he is kind unto the unthankful and to the evil.

(Psalms 37:8) Cease from anger, and forsake wrath: fret not thyself in any wise to do evil.

---

[18] 1Pe 2:23 NCV

(James 1:22) But be ye doers of the word, and not hearers only, deceiving your own selves.

9

LOVE IS PROFITABLE

For bodily exercise profiteth little: but godliness is profitable unto all things, having promise of the life that now is, and of that which is to come (1 Timothy 4:8).

Our great God and Father provides benefits and rewards for His children. These numerous blessings are the visible expression of His goodness and kindness. They reveal the fullness of our great salvation. This salvation, according to the Greek word "sozo," translated "save," includes:

- Deliverance
- Protection
- Healing
- Wholeness [1]

It encompasses everything that pertains to life.
The path to God's bountiful blessings is described by

---

[1] G4982, *Strong's*

the apostle Paul in 1 Timothy 4:8. He says:

Godliness is profitable for all things. [2]

When something is profitable, it brings noticeable gain, and in this Scripture, the profit, or gain, is for "all things." The *New English Bible* explains the expression "for all things" by speaking of benefits "without limit." Other translations proclaim blessings:

- in every respect [3]
- in every way [4]
- in all directions [5]

What tremendous promises! God's unending generosity blesses us in this life as well as "in the world to come." [6]

Ordinarily, in a financial transaction, we do not invest in the stock of one company expecting to receive dividends from two companies. But in God's kingdom, an investment in godliness graces our lives with blessings on earth AND in heaven. **The reward of godliness begins today and extends into eternity.**

What is godliness? I believe godliness is obedience to

---

[2] 1Ti 4:8, NKJV
[3] WEY
[4] RSV
[5] MOF
[6] Author's paraphrase

108

God's New Covenant law of love. If we ignore or forsake God's command of love, we do not live godly lives. We will not reveal God's loving nature and we cannot influence others.

The gospel of salvation is not perpetuated if God's love does not lead our lives.

Many New Testament writers urge us to obey God's principle of love. The apostle Paul highlights love as a continual command, an unending debt, saying:

Owe no man any thing, but to love one another. [7]

The voice of Peter declares God's love is a fervent, intense, and glowing fire. [8] These directives magnify the importance of earnest and constant obedience.

THE ENEMY OF LOVE

When we dedicate ourselves to this principle of love, God's blessings pour into our lives. However, we undermine and thwart these benefits if we refuse to love others.

Anger, malice, bitterness, and other evil works frustrate the profit and reward of godliness, and they give

---

[7] Ro 13:8
[8] 1Pe 4:8

the devil an opportunity to defeat us.

Many tenets of religion cast the devil as an imaginary foe, but the Scripture reveals the reality of this adversary. The apostle Peter exhorts us to:

Be sober, be vigilant; because your adversary the devil, as a roaring lion, walketh about, seeking whom he may devour. [9]

Truly, there is a devil who destroys lives. When we fail to walk in love, we open the door to the operation of his kingdom. Jesus spoke of Satan and his kingdom throughout the Gospels. He referred to him as a:

thief [who] does not come except to steal, and to kill, and to destroy. [10]

This powerful Scripture reveals the work of Satan, but there is good news for every Christian! The death and resurrection of our Lord Jesus Christ defeated this evil foe! **God triumphed over Satan and his kingdom through the cross.** [11] Today, when Satan plots against us, the power of God enforces his defeat!

---

[9] 1Pe 5:8
[10] Jn 10:10 NKJV
[11] Col 2:15

A DEFEATED FOE

I love God's Word in Exodus 23:22. In this verse, God says:

_____

I will be an enemy to your enemies and an adversary to your adversaries. [12]

_____

_____

[12] NKJV

What a marvelous revelation! The enemy of man is also the enemy of God. Our great God conquered our enemy, Satan, through Jesus, His "only begotten Son" [13] and by the mighty power of the name of Jesus, Satan is "under our feet." [14]

In Christ, he is bound, and we are victorious.

HEALING AND PROSPERITY

Although Satan has been defeated by the risen Christ, he has not been eliminated. One day, he will be cast into the lake of fire to be tormented forever. [15] Until that time, he attempts to deceive those who do not recognize the authority of Christ. **He perverts truth, promotes doubt, and sanctions persecution in order to consume us.**

Jesus opened our eyes to one avenue of Satan's destructive power when he healed the woman with the spirit of infirmity. He said:

Ought not this woman, being a daughter of Abraham, whom Satan hath bound, lo, these eighteen years, be loosed from this bond on the sabbath day? [16]

Jesus clearly established the sickness in her body as

---

[13] Jn 3:16
[14] Eph 1:20-23
[15] Rev 20:10
[16] Lk 13:16

satanic bondage.

The apostle Peter repeated this truth when he preached to the household of Cornelius. He proclaimed:

Jesus ... went about doing good, and healing all that were oppressed of the devil. [17]

This identifies Satan as the procurator of disease, but it also magnifies the healing power of God manifested in Jesus' life.

When God's power heals the sick, He is glorified.

Religious fervor often speaks to the contrary, lauding disease as being for the glory of God, but the testimony of the Word of God does not validate this declaration. The multitudes did not applaud sickness or reverence disease. They brought sick people to Jesus and glorified God when He healed them. They glorified God for healing the lame, blind, deaf, and maimed. [18] The crowds honored God because Jesus healed a paralytic. [19] The woman with the spirit of infirmity also glorified God when she was able to stand up straight. [20]

Healing always honors God.

---

[17] Ac 10:38
[18] Mt. 15:30-31
[19] Mt 9:6-8
[20] Lk 13:13

God is also magnified when He supplies our material needs. Satan, the god of this world, not only promotes disease, but he devours by poverty and lack as well.

Our God is a good God who abundantly provides our needs! This is the testimony of the apostle Paul.

But my God shall supply ALL your need according to His riches in glory by Christ Jesus. [21]

The psalmist corroborates this with the announcement:

They that seek the Lord shall not want ANY good thing. [22]

He also said:

The Lord is my shepherd; I shall NOT want. [23]

These three witnesses leave no doubt that God wants His children to prosper.

[21] Php 4:19, author's emphasis
[22] Ps 34:10, author's emphasis
[23] Ps 23:1, author's emphasis

114

However, this prosperity does not promote greed or sanction selfishness. Instead, it embraces a living God who:

---

blesses us with everything we need to enjoy life. [24]

It highlights a loving Father who will never leave us or forsake us. [25] He supplies our daily bread. [26]
He has promised:

You will always have everything you need and plenty left over to share with others. [27]

This is God's bountiful harvest for those who give cheerfully and generously. It is God's plan of prosperity!

ABOVE ALL THINGS

These blessings from God, our Father, are not maybe-so, could-be, or cross-your-fingers benefits. They are God's will!
The apostle John substantiates this truth when he proclaims:

---

[24] 1Ti 6:17 CEV
[25] Heb 13:5
[26] Mt 6:11;Lk 11:3;Ps 37:25
[27] 2Co 9:8 NLT

Beloved, I wish above all things that thou mayest prosper and be in health, even as thy soul prospereth. [28]

This word from the Holy Spirit is very significant! **God wants us to prosper and walk in health "above all things."** I love the phrase "above all things." When a desire is "above all things," it is first in importance.

In earlier years as Wayne and I travelled teaching God's Word, we left someone in charge of our household. She was responsible for many important tasks, but nothing was more significant than giving time and attention to our

---

[28] 3Jn 1:2

dog. "Above all things" we wanted our dog to be comfortable and fed on time.

We appreciated a clean kitchen and freshly vacuumed carpet, yet our priority was the need of our dog. In our household, she was "above all things."

Now, in order to prosper and walk in health "above all things," our soul must prosper. This very important revelation is explained when the apostle John commended Gaius for walking in truth. [29] Obviously, it was Gaius' obedience to truth that caused his soul to prosper.

But what is truth? Jesus said God's Word is truth. [30]

Therefore, if we honor God's Word, our soul prospers, and we enjoy God's abundant blessings. When we reverently obey God's law of love, every day is a "day of rewards."

Yes, godliness is profitable in all things!

Scriptures for Meditation:

(1 Timothy 4:8) For bodily exercise profiteth little: but godliness is profitable unto all things, having promise of the life that now is, and of that which is to come.

(3 John 1:2-3) Beloved, I wish above all things that thou mayest prosper and be in health, even as thy soul prospereth. For I rejoiced greatly, when the brethren came and testified of the truth that is in thee, even as thou walkest in the truth.

---

[29] 3Jn 1:3-4
[30] Jn 17:17

10

SUMMARY
LOVE IS VICTORIOUS!

Love is a decision. Love is an action. Love is a response. Love does not speak loud, angry words. It is not filled with jealous resentment or overbearing envy.

The love of God is far different than these physical and emotional forces. God's love is mercifully longsuffering, unselfish, and kind. Like a sculptor, it creates a masterpiece, breathing serenity into our soul. It is God's greatest gift.

This gift of love must direct our lives.

It must dominate our flesh and capture our thoughts. How can we tell if God's love is leading the parade of our heart? Here is our simple answer:

We act right, live right, do right and speak correctly.

We repent quickly too. Thank God for repentance! I believe in repentance! When I confess my sins, they are forgiven, and the hand of God's love comforts me. I am so very glad!

God's great love has provided us with:

---

all spiritual blessings in heavenly places. [1]

Oh, how good is God, our Father! He has given us everything, yes, all that we need through His Son. As we surrender to Him, we are confident that His blessings manifest in our lives.

The great hymn eloquently penned by J. H. Sammis emphasizes our submission to God's will. Oh, that we would listen carefully as we sing.

"When we walk with the Lord in the light of His Word, what a glory He sheds on our way! While we do His good-will, He abides with us still, and with all who will trust and obey." [2]

Our songwriter correctly advises, "Walk with the Lord, in the light of His Word." He further states, "Do His good-will," and then he declares, "Trust and obey." **This is the road to glory, the path into God's presence and His benefits.**

Trust and obey! Again and again, we hear this grand refrain in our heart.

It reminds us of Israel's glorious victory at Jericho. When Israel was instructed to cross the Jordan River into the Promised Land, Jericho was the first major city, the first

---

[1] Eph 1:3

[2] "Trust and Obey," Words by John H. Sammis, 1887; Music by Daniel B. Towner <http://www.cyberhymnal.org/htm/t/r/trstobey.htm>, Accessed 24 May 2011.

major enemies, God's people would encounter. History records that the walls of Jericho could accommodate two chariots riding abreast. What a wall!

God told Joshua that Jericho's walls would fall, but He gave specific instructions that must be obeyed. God's people must walk around the walls of Jericho once a day for six days. On the seventh day, they must compass the city seven times and then with the sound of the trumpet and a great shout, the walls would fall. [3]

If Israel obeyed His directions, there would be great victory. Israel could choose to remain by the Jordan River, gazing towards the city of Jericho, hoping for victory, or they could obey God. If they did not act or respond to the instructions of the Lord, the walls would stand. The enemy would remain in the land. The answer for Israel was to trust and obey.

The door to victory always opens as we obediently trust God. The central directive of this trust is voiced by Jesus in John 13:39. Here, He instructed His disciples to:

---

love one another. [4]

This principle is the heart of the New Covenant and the foundation of success.

There is no bigger testing ground for this loving decree than in our home. Our dedication to God and His Word must begin there.

Yet often, within the walls of home we relinquish our faith and draw back from the great principles of love. It is there, however, that the command of love must first pour from our spirit. At home, our voice must reflect our trust in God and our actions demonstrate His care.

As we walk in God's love, we can expect His power to

---

[3] Jos 6:1-5
[4] Jn 13:34

rescue our marriage and influence our children. I know this is true! After many years of marriage, the love of God continues to work mightily in my husband, Wayne, and I. Certainly, God's love does not fail!

We must continually meditate on God's words of love, stirring our spirit until His love dominates our body and our soul. The value of this meditation cannot be overlooked. If we are sick, we diligently study the Scriptures on healing. We read them over and over because we want the power of God's Word and His Spirit in our lives. In the same way, we deposit God's command of love in our heart. Faithful meditation enables our spirit to respond in love.

This meditation draws us to God, not for an occasional glance at truth, but for a steadfast look.

As we focus on the Scripture, reflecting on every word, the Holy Spirit teaches us. He strengthens our spirit until the love of God in our heart acts and does and gives and provides.

This is the key to victory. When we obey God's loving command, we are "exceedingly abundantly" [5] blessed. Everything prospers with God's love!

---

[5] Eph 3:20

OUTLINES THAT TEACH

Chapter outlines for study and review

1

THE BEGINNING
THE LOVE OF GOD IS SO BIG!

I. The Love of God
    A. "God SO loved the world."
       John 3:16
    B. God loves us with GREAT love.
       Ephesians 2:5
II. The Provision of God
    A. God gave His only begotten Son.
       John 3:16
       1 John 4:9
    B. Jesus sacrificed His life.
       1 John 3:16
III. The Promise of Eternal Life
    A. God offers eternal life.
       John 3:16
       John 4:14
       John 5:24
       Romans 6:23
    B. Eternal life is abundant life.
       John 10:10
IV. The Way to Eternal Life
    A. Jesus is life.
       1 John 1:2
       John 14:6

B. All men can receive eternal life.
John 3:16
John 3:36
C. We must believe in the resurrection.
Romans 10:9-10
D. We must confess Jesus as Lord.
Romans 10:9-10
E. We can have eternal life today!
2 Corinthians 6:2
V. The Nature of Man
A. All men are spirit, soul, and body.
1 Thessalonians 5:23
B. The spirit must be reborn.
John 3:6
2 Corinthians 5:17

2

THE COMMAND
LOVE ONE ANOTHER

I.   The Influence of Love
    A. Love reveals God's disciples.
        John 13:35
    B. We ought to love others.
        1 John 4:11

II.   Jesus, God's Gift of Love
    A. Isaiah announces Jesus' birth and His death.
        Isaiah 9:6
        Isaiah 53:3,5
    B. The psalmist envisions Jesus' death.
        Psalm 22:16
    C. Job proclaims the resurrection.
        Job 19:25

III.   The Place of the Old Covenant
    A. The Old Covenant contains many commandments.
        Exodus 20:1-17
    B. The Old Covenant sacrifices could not take away sin.
        Hebrews 10:1-4
    C. Jesus fulfilled the Old Covenant.
        Matthew 5:17

IV.   The Provision of the New Covenant
- A. The New Covenant manifests as the Old Covenant is completed.
  Hebrews 8:13
- B. In the New Covenant, the blood of Jesus blotted out sin.
  Acts 3:19
  Hebrews 9:26
  Hebrews 10:17
  1 John 3:5
- C. The New Covenant unveils one law to fulfill many.
  Romans 13:8-10
  Galatians 5:14

V.   The New Law of Love
- A. Jesus revealed the new commandment of love.
  John 13:34
- B. The love of God is in the spirit of man.
  Romans 5:5
- C. We must love others.
  John 13:35
  1 John 4:7-8

THE DILEMMA
FLESH LIKES

I.   The Greatest Attribute of God
        1 Corinthians 13:13

II.   The Way of Love
    A. God's love is not a feeling.
      Strong's ,G5368, comparison
    B. God's love is more than words.
      1 Corinthians 13:1
    C. God's love exceeds knowledge.
      1 Corinthians 13:2
    D. God's love is greater than sacrifice.
      1 Corinthians 13:3

III.   The Influence of the Flesh
    A. The flesh contradicts the Spirit
      Romans 7:18
      Galatians 5:17
    B. The flesh must be crucified
      Romans 12:1
      Galatians 5:24
      1 Corinthians 9:27
    C. We walk in the Spirit.
      Galatians 5:16,18,25

IV.   Victory Over the Flesh
    A. The Holy Spirit helps us.
      Romans 8:13

B. The love of God constrains us.
   2 Corinthians 5:14
C. Jesus gives victory.
   Romans 7:24-25

4

THE PREPARATION
DAY AND NIGHT

I.   A Time For Meditation
     A. Meditation defined.
        H1897, *Strong's*
     B. Meditation is continual.
        Joshua 1:8
     C. Meditation prepares us for success.
        Psalm 1:2-3
     D. We reject ungodly counsel.
        Psalm 1:1

II.   The Path of Meditation
     A. Christians listen carefully.
        Deuteronomy 28:1
        Proverbs 4:20
     B. Christians are "doers."
        Deuteronomy 28:1,13
        James 1:22

III. The Dimensions of Love
     A. We love God.
        Matthew 22:37
        Mark 12:30
        Luke 10:27
     B. We love one another.
        John 13:34
        John 15:12,17
        Romans 13:8

2 John 1:5
- C. We love our enemies.
  Matthew 5:44
  Luke 6:27
- D. We love our husband or wife.
  Ephesians 5:28,33
  Titus 2:4

IV. The Way of Success
- A. We meditate on God's Word.
  Joshua 1:8
- B. We study God's Word.
  2 Timothy 2:15
- C. We choose love.
  Ephesians 1:4 CEV

5

THE EXPLANATION
LOVE IS

I. The Way of Longsuffering
    A. Love is longsuffering.
       1 Corinthians 13:4
    B. Longsuffering displays restraint and mercy.
       Definition, *Vine's*
    C. God is longsuffering.
       Exodus 34:61
    D. Time is the gift of longsuffering.
       2 Peter 3:9

II. The Path of Kindness
    A. Love is kind.
       1 Corinthians 13:4
    B. Kindness and longsuffering work together.
       1 Corinthians 13:4
    C. Kindness manifests through words and deeds.
       1 John 3:18
    D. Kindness faces "evil" with good.
       Romans 12:21

III. The Road to Seemly Behavior
    A. Love is seemly.
       1 Corinthians 13:5
    B. Seemly behavior defines our position and
       character.
       Definition, *Webster's*, 1959

      C. We are children of God.
           John 1:12
           1 John 3:2
      D. We imitate God.
           Matthew 5:48
           Ephesians 5:1
      E. Jesus reveals the Father.
           John 14:9

IV.   The Direction of Unselfishness
      A. Love is not selfish.
           1 Corinthians 13:5
      B. Love values others.
           Philippians 2:3
      C. Love defers to others.
           Romans 12:10

6

THE EXCEPTIONS
WE CAN BE CHANGED

I.   The Perilous Road of Envy
   - A. Envy is dangerous.
     1 Corinthians 13:4
   - B. The Philistines envy Isaac.
     Genesis 26:12-14
   - C. Joseph is envied by his brothers.
     Genesis 37:3-8

II.   The Solution For Boasting
   - A. We do not magnify ourselves.
     1 Corinthians 13:4
     Philippians 2:3
   - B. We value others.
     Romans 12:10
     Philippians 2:3
   - C. We are servants.
     Matthew 20:27
     Galatians 5:13

III. The Response to Anger
   - A. We are not easily provoked.
     1 Corinthians 13:5
     James 1:19
   - B. We will not retaliate.
     Romans 12:17
     1 Peter 2:23

C. We speak gently.
   Proverbs 15:1
IV.   The Way To Change
   2 Corinthians 3:16

7

THE ANGER
I'M MAD

I. The Words of Our Lord
    A. Jesus instructs us to forgive.
       Mark 11:25
       Luke 6:37
    B. The Lord's Prayer teaches us to forgive.
       Matthew 6:12

II. The Principles of Forgiveness
    A. We "do not yield" to anger.
       Ephesians 4:26
    B. We overlook offenses.
       1 Corinthians 13:5
    C. We are kind.
       Ephesians 4:32
    D. We forgive quickly.
       Ephesians 4:26

III. The Forgiveness of God
    A. God blots out sin.
       Isaiah 43:25
       Acts 3:19
    B. God does not remember sin.
       Hebrews 8:12

IV. The Provision of Repentance
    A. We confess sin.
       1 John 1:9

B. We are cleansed and forgiven.
   1 John 1:9
C. The blood of Jesus cleanses us.
   1 John 1:7

V. The Walk of Forgiveness
   A. We imitate God.
      Ephesians 5:1
   B. We forgive over and over again.
      Matthew 18:21-22
   C. We seek reconciliation.
      Galatians 6:1
   D. We strive for peace.
      Romans 12:18

8

THE RESPONSE
DO UNTO OTHERS

I.   Two Kinds of Love
    A. *Agape* is a decision.
    B. *Phileo* is a feeling.
       Comparison, G5368, *Strong's*
II.   The Call of Love
    A. We are doers.
       Colossians 3:17
       James 1:22
    B. We respond in word and deed.
       James 1:27
       James 2:16
       1 John 3:17
    C. We speak graciously.
       Ephesians 4:29
    D. We do not complain.
       Philippians 2:14
    E. We overcome evil works with good deeds.
       Psalm 37:8
       Romans 12:20-21
III. The Help of God
    A. God is the Greater One.
       1 John 4:4

B. We are God's temple.
   1 Corinthians 3:16
   1 Corinthians 6:19
C. The Holy Spirit leads us.
   Romans 8:14
   James 4:8
D. God's judgment is just.
   1 Peter 2:23

9

THE REWARD
LOVE IS PROFITABLE

I.   The Principles of Godliness
   - A. Godliness is gain in all things.
     1 Timothy 4:8
   - B. Godliness profits today and into eternity.
     1 Timothy 4:8
   - C. Our godly lives manifest God's love.
     Romans 13:8
     1 Peter 4:8

II.   The Tyranny of Satan
   - A. Satan seeks to destroy man.
     John 10:10
     1 Peter 5:8
   - B. Satan destroys man with sickness.
     Luke 13:16
     Acts 10:38
   - C. Satan is defeated.
     Ephesians 1:20-23
     Colossians 2:15
   - D. Satan is "tormented day and night."
     Revelation 20:10

III. The Provision of God
   - A. God heals the sick.
     Acts 10:38

B. Healing glorifies God.
   Matthew 9:8
   Matthew 15:30-31
   Luke 13:13
C. God desires to prosper His children.
   Psalm 23:1
   Psalm 34:10
   Philippians 4:19

IV. The Power of Obedience
A. God desires prosperity "above all things."
   3 John 1:2
B. First, our soul must prosper.
   3 John 1:2
C. Our soul prospers through obedience to truth.
   3 John 1:3-4

ABOUT THE AUTHOR

Reverend Becky Combee has been teaching Bible principles in home and church groups for over thirty years. She is known for her Bible knowledge, unique humor, and atypical sketches.

Ordained in 1996 under the ministry of Pastor Reggie Scarborough of Family Worship Center in Lakeland, Florida, she ministers the Word of God in her local church, across the United States, and around the world.

Becky Combee is a native Floridian. She and her husband, Wayne, have been married for fifty years and have two children who assist them in ministry giving computer expertise, photographic skills, and office administration.

Becky and Wayne Combee are committed to the Word of God as truth and the Holy Spirit as God who reveals truth. It is their heart's desire to clearly define the Word of God to all who will hear in our world.

More information about Becky Combee Ministries, Inc., can be found at www.beckycombeeministries.com.

www.ingramcontent.com/pod-product-compliance
Lightning Source LLC
Chambersburg PA
CBHW072011040426
42447CB00009B/1589